Implementing High Quality Collaborative Teams

Creating and Sustaining a Collaborative Culture

Michael J. Wasta Ph.D.

Title ID: 7284062
ISBN-13: 978-1548319366

DEDICATION

This book is dedicated to my first teachers, Rita and Joseph Wasta and all of the hard working teachers with whom I have worked in a career that spans five decades. The impact a great teacher can have on the lives of his or her students is profound.

CONTENTS

ACKNOWLEDGMENTS

The author would like to thank the following people and organizations for their assistance in making this book possible:

Dr. Douglas Reeves, founder and president of Creative Leadership Solutions, for his unwavering support and encouragement

The Bristol, Connecticut Public Schools with leadership from Deputy Superintendent Dr. Susan Kalt Moreau and the Windsor, Connecticut Public Schools under the leadership of Superintendent, Dr. Craig Cook, for staying the course on collaboration in the face of tremendous challenges

Norwich Free Academy (CT) under the leadership of David Klein, Head of School, and the Southington, Connecticut Public Schools under the leadership of Superintendent, Timothy Connellan, and Assistant Superintendent, Steven Madancy, for their thoughtful, comprehensive approach to expanding collaborative work cultures in their schools

INTRODUCTION

This book contains a great deal of information about how a school or district can move to a more collaborative work culture.

All of this information is useless, however, unless the people in a particular school or district can integrate this information into their existing culture.

The work of schools is highly contextual. What works in one school or district frequently fails when copied wholesale into another system. For this reason the reader will see following every major idea or suggestion, space for the reader to write down his/her thoughts or reflections. There are likely to be suggestions presented that can be improved upon, and others that your school/district is simply not ready to embrace – yet. In other words, the plan for moving to a more collaborative culture has to be your plan, not this author's.

The vision here is that a small, core team be trained to deal with the complex conditions that need to be confronted and surmounted in order to take the collaborative work of educators to a level that can have significant impact on student outcomes. This team is not meant to replace an external expert on collaboration. Initially, at least, such expertise is almost always needed. Regardless of the expertise of the external consultant however it remains a fact that the school or district must develop expertise in implementing the particular form of collaboration in their unique situation. In other words, the external consultant may be an expert on Professional Learning Communities (PLC's) or Data Teams but the internal staff must become experts on implementing the process in their particular situation. Without this, collaborative teams like many, many other initiatives in education frequently wither and die due to the fact that there is insufficient planning to insure deep, sustained implementation.

The training material contained in this book will arm an Implementation Team with the information and tools needed to improve the chance that this initiative will become imbedded into the fabric of the district or school and become; "just the way we do things here".

This Book contains:

- Information documenting the widespread and long standing evidence of the efficacy of improving educator collaboration
- Documented elements that are related to more successful collaboration initiatives
- A protocol that has been found effective for teams to follow as they move toward more sophisticated collaboration involving a focus on changing adult behaviors
- A description of a dynamic planning process to replace the rigid process that frequently characterizes team planning
- Tools and a process to assess the progression of collaborative teams over time
- Information regarding implementation barriers and pitfalls with suggestions on how to surmount
- Suggestions to insure long lasting implementation
- Development of an implementation plan for your school or district

Armed with the information above and with periodic external support as needed, this team can oversee the implementation of a collaborative work initiative over time and with a degree of expertise rarely seen in education initiatives.

Evidence That Supports the Efficacy of Educator Collaboration to Improve Student Outcomes

"The research indicates that...", "The literature says...", "The evidence shows..."- How many times have we heard such comments from a presenter, consultant or leader as he or she attempts to convince a group of educators to take a particular course of action or implement a particular program? Rarely is the research, literature or evidence actually produced. It is perhaps a sad commentary on the education profession that this lack of evidence is rarely challenged. Major initiatives in the education field are frequently undertaken when the available evidence of efficacy is weak or even entirely absent. Dogma frequently trumps data and facts.

The purpose of this section is to arm those charged with deep implementation of high quality collaborative teams with at least a portion of the vast volume of research that has been developed over the past 30 years. The result of this research, conducted in schools of every stripe and in countries throughout the world, has been remarkably consistent in documenting the efficacy of this work. But it should not be good enough just to make a statement like this. Informed, thoughtful implementers should actually know what this research evidence is or at least some of it. Therefore, we begin our journey with a review of some of the most compelling evidence available. Although we will deal with summaries of these studies, virtually all of those cited are freely available on the Internet if one wishes to read the entire study.

One last comment before we begin - A frequent comment when research is cited in support of a practice or program is; "You can find research to support anything." While there may be some truth to this statement, it should not be left unchallenged. To those who say this, a response may be, " If you can find research that presents different conclusions than these, please present it and we can have an informed debate prior to coming to a conclusion."

We begin our exploration by examining a number of empirical studies concerning the efficacy of teacher collaboration for improving student outcomes.

Next, we will review a number of more anecdotal situations where schools relate the experience they had after implementing various forms of collaboration. There are literally hundreds of such papers available and only a sample is presented here.

Third, we review the opinions of a number of "experts" both within and outside of education with regard to the positive effects of collaboration.

Finally, we cite the positions of a number of educational organizations regarding the issue.

What we are looking for here is a "preponderance of evidence", to borrow a phrase from the legal profession. The information presented here spans all grade levels, different countries, at least 20 years and different political philosophies.

Empirical Data

Study Summaries

"A Theoretical and Empirical Investigation of Teacher Collaboration for School Improvement and Student Achievement in Public Elementary Schools." Goddard, Y.L. & Goddard, R.D. & Tschannen-Moran, M. (2007). Teachers College Record, 109, (4), pp. 877-896.

This study took place in a large mid western school district (47 elementary schools, 452 teachers, 2,536 fourth grade students).

Student achievement was measured by performance on the state mandated assessment. Teacher collaboration was measured by a survey assessing teacher level of collaboration. Findings: Teacher collaboration was a statistically significant predictor of variability among students in both mathematics and reading achievement. A one-standard deviation increase in the extent to which teachers collaborated on school improvement was associated with a .08 standard deviation increase in average school mathematics achievement and a .07 standard deviation increase in average reading achievement. This is a moderate correlation.

"Moving the Learning of Teaching Closer to Practice: Teacher Education Implications of School-Based Inquiry Teams." Gallimore, R., Ermeling, B.A., Saunders, W.M., & Goldenberg, C. (2009). The Elementary School Journal. 109(5), pp. 537-553.

This five year quasi-experimental investigation across nine Title I elementary schools in a large southern California district compared achievement over time in schools implementing learning teams to control schools not implementing learning teams.

Schools implementing learning teams started out well below the district average in mathematics and reading but surpassed comparison schools and the district average by the end of 5 years.

"Instructional Leadership: A Pathway to Teacher Collaboration and Student Achievement." Miller, R.J., Goddard, Y.L., Goddard, R. Texas A&M University. Larsen, R. University of Virginia, and Jacob, R.,

14

University of Michigan. Paper presented at the University Council for Educational Administration Convention, October 2010, New Orleans, LA.

Data were obtained from 1605 teachers in 96 elementary schools where principals were participating in a randomized control trial to assess the efficacy of a widely disseminated professional development program for school leaders. Using structural equation modeling it was found that there was a significant direct effect of instructional leadership on teacher collaboration and a significant effect of collaboration on student achievement. The indirect effect of leadership on student achievement through teacher collaboration was significant.

"Teacher Collaboration in Instructional Teams and Student Achievement." Ronfeldt, M., Farmer, S.O., McQueen, K., University of Michigan. Grissom, J.A., Vanderbilt University. American Educational Research Journal. June, 2015. Vol.52, No.3, pp.475-514.

This study involved a survey and administrative data from over 9,000 teachers in 336 Miami-Dade County public schools over a 2 year period investigating the kinds of collaborations that existed in instructional teams and whether those collaborations could predict student achievement. Findings revealed that schools and teachers that engage in better quality collaboration had better achievement gains in reading and math. Teacher quality also improved in schools with better quality collaboration.

"The Missing Link in School Reform." Leana, C.R., Stanford Social Innovation Review. Fall 2011. Stanford University.

This study took place in the New York City public schools between 2005 and 2007. It involved 1,000 4th and 5th grade teachers from 130 elementary schools. The study measured students' math growth over a period of one year. The study also measured teachers' math ability and the degree to which they collaborated with their peers.

Findings: Students of high math ability teachers outperformed those of low-ability teachers. Students of teachers who had stronger ties to their peers (collaboration) showed the highest gains in math. **Even low-ability math teachers can perform as well as teachers of average ability if they have strong social capital (collaboration) with their peers.**

"Tracing the Effects of Teacher Inquiry on Classroom Practice." Ermeling, B.A., Journal of Teaching and Teacher Education, 2010, #26, pp. 377-388.

The focus of this study was four high school science teachers in a private, comprehensive, urban high school in southern California where the teachers were trained and guided in a collaborative process focused on changing instruction to improve student outcomes. It documented changes in teacher practice (videotapes) and also documented improvement in student outcomes.

"Does Professional Community Affect the Teachers' Work and Student Experiences in Restructuring Schools." Louis, Karen Seashore, & Marks, Helen. Paper presented at the annual meeting of the American Educational Research Association (New York, NY, April 8-12, 1996)

Eight elementary, eight middle, and eight high schools were selected. Surveys were completed by 910 teachers and the instructional practices of 144 teachers were studied. The school professional community was found to be most characteristic of elementary schools and least characteristic of high schools. Findings strongly support the conceptual model posited, that the organization of teachers' work in ways that promote professional community has significant effects on the organization of classrooms for learning and the academic performance of students.

"Collective Responsibility for Learning and Its Effects on Gains in Achievement for Early Secondary School Students." Lee, V.E., & Smith, J.B., 1996, American Journal of Education, Vol.104, #2., pp.103-147.

A nationally representative sample of 11,692 high school sophomores in 820 U.S. High schools and 9,904 of those students' teachers was used. Organizational effects were evaluated on students' gains in achievement in math, reading, science, and social studies between 8th and 10th grade. The study focused on 3 constructs measuring the organization of teachers' work: collective responsibility for student learning, staff cooperation and control over classroom and school work conditions. Results were very consistent: achievement gains were significantly higher in schools where teachers took collective responsibility for students' academic success or failure rather than blaming students for their own failure. Achievement gains were also higher in schools with more cooperation among staff.

"The Impact of Collaborative Continuing Professional Development on Classroom Teaching and Learning – A Review." Paper produced by The EPPI Centre Social Science Research Unit, Institute of Education, University of London. 2016.

This review compares research studies comparing the impact of collaborative and individually oriented professional development (PD). From a pool of 5,505 titles the group narrowed the field to 81 studies that met their criteria.

Findings: Individually oriented PD showed relatively low impact on teacher practice and student learning. Collaboratively oriented PD showed consistent effectiveness in bringing about changes in teaching and learning.

Anecdotal Data

Hudson High School, Hudson, St. Croix County, Wisconsin.

"Getting Better All The Time", American School Board Journal. May, 2011. Vol. 198, # 5, p. 38-39.

Teachers working collaboratively reduced the failure rate from 20.5% to 4.7%.

Urban High School, New York, New York.

International High School, Queens, New York.

Hodgson Vocational Technical High School, Newark, Delaware.

"The Reciprocal Influence of Teacher-Learning, Teaching Practice, School Restructuring and Student Learning Outcomes". Jacqueline Ancess. Teachers College Record, Vol. 102, #3, 2000. p. 590-619.

Three high schools all serving at-risk students dramatically improved graduation rates, course pass rates, college admission rates and academic course-taking rates.

"The findings of this study suggest that teachers inquiry into their own practice with a particular set of students for whom they have set particular goals can be a rich source of teacher learning and a powerful opportunity for improving student performance."

Philadelphia Public Schools

Cincinnati Public Schools

"Developing Communities of Instructional Practice: Lessons from Cincinnati and Philadelphia". Johathan A. Supovitz and Jolley Bruce Christman. Policy Briefs, Nov. 2003, RB 39. Consortium for Policy Research in Education, p. 1-11.

Large-scale implementation of teacher teams was studied.

"Thus, in both cities, only where communities focused on changing the instructional practices of their members was there measurable improvement in student learning."

"In both Philadelphia and Cincinnati there was evidence to suggest that those communities that did engage in structured, sustained and supported instructional discussions and that investigated the relationships between instructional practices and student work produced significant gains in student learning."

Faubion Elementary School, Portland, Oregon

"Vital Signs". Grace Rubenstein, Edutopia, June 2006, Vol. 2, #4, p. 20-23.

The focus of this report was student achievement gains in a small elementary school. The percentage of students meeting reading standards moved from 66% to 90%.

The percentage of students meeting math standards moved from 71% to 92%.

Teacher teams used common assessments to monitor student performance, and met weekly to collaborate and plan instruction.

Urban High School

"Professional Learning Communities as a Leadership Strategy to Drive Math Success in an Urban High School Serving Low-Income Students: A Case Study." Kristin Shawn Huggins, James Joseph Scheurich and James Morgan. Journal of Education for Students at Risk, April-June 2011, Vol. 16, #2, p. 67-88.

Structured, data rich collaboration between 6 teachers and 3 administrators raised math achievement from 58% meeting standards to 78% meeting standards in one year.

Penasquitos Elementary School, San Diego, California

Levey Middle School, Southfield, Michigan

"Promises Kept", Richard DuFour, Rebecca DuFour, Damon Lopez and Anthony Muchammad. Journal of Staff Development, Summer 2006, Vol. 27,#3, p. 53-56.

Lowest performing elementary school in San Diego became one of the highest performing in California and earned national awards for excellence.

The Middle school more than doubled the percentage of students meeting State English and LA standards. Math performance moved above the state average.

Grade level or common course teams focused on issues of student learning, using evidence of student performance to guide changes in teacher practice. In each case a compelling moral purpose was paired with the technical practices.

Marylin Avenue Elementary School, Livermore, California

"Data Use: Data-Driven Decision Making Takes a Big Picture View of the Needs of Teachers and Students." Victoria L. Bernahardt. Journal of Staff Development. 2009, Vol. 30, # 1, p. 24-27.

In this 500 pupil elementary school with 75% poverty, 34% mobility, and a high population of non-English speaking students, student achievement improved at every grade level in every subject. Collaborative teams of teachers used time to discuss student assessment results and student work to identify how they needed to change instructional strategies to get improved results. They kept the collaborative time sacred and modeled how to use the time and data effectively.

Adlai Stevenson High School, Lincolnshire, Illinois

"Working Smarter by Working Together". Vaishali Honawar. Education Week, April 2, 2008, Vol. 27, #31, p. 25-27.

It was at this school that Richard DuFour pioneered Professional Learning Communities over 30 years ago. This school has continued the practice since then and has achieved and maintained outstanding performance in a very large high school.

Blue Valley High School, Overland Park, Kansas

"Up Close and Personal: Data Review Creates an 'Aha' Moment for Suburban Teachers". Joan Richardson, Results, National Staff

Development Council. March 2005.

Forty percent of the students had one or more D's or F's as a final grade. Teachers created collaborative teams for Math, English, Science and Social Studies. In meetings teachers collaborated regarding common assessments, specific goals, and improved instruction. They cut the number of D's and F's in half over a 6 year period.

Archer Elementary School, Greensboro, North Carolina

Hunter Elementary School, Raleigh, North Carolina

North Elementary School, North Carolina

"Promoting a Collaborative Professional Culture in Three Elementary Schools That Have Beaten the Odds." David Straha. Elementary School Journal. Nov. 2003, Vol. 104, # 2, p. 127-146.

These schools made dramatic gains in student achievement. Students at or above grade level in reading and math went from 46.2% in 1997 to 75.6% in 2002. They implemented weekly grade level teams that used common assessment data to monitor student performance, and collaboratively created instructional strategies. Teachers linked all professional development to daily practice. Teachers developed a very high collaborative attitude.

Woodsedge Middle School*, Houston, Texas

*Pseudonym

"Powerful Learning: Creating Learning Communities in Urban School Reform." Joy Phillips, Journal of Curriculum and Supervision, Spring 2003, Vol. 18, # 3, p. 240-258.

At this large middle school (1425 students) in grades 6-8, we see how in 3 years they moved from an Acceptable Rating (50% + of students meeting state standards on reading, math, science, writing and social studies assessments to Exemplary Rating (90%+ of students meeting state standards on reading, math, science, writing and social studies assessments.

They used high quality professional development, shared leadership, collaboration imbedded in context. The focus was on improving teacher learning.

Expert Opinion

"The most successful corporation of the future will be a learning organization." Senge, P. (1990 p. 4). The Fifth Discipline: The Art and Practice of the Learning Organization. New York: Currency Doubleday.

"Every enterprise has to become a learning institution (and) a teaching institution. Organizations that build in a continuous learning in jobs will dominate the 21st century." Drucker, P. (1992 p. 108). Managing for the Future: The 1990s and Beyond. New York: Truman Talley Books.

"The new problem of change ...is what would it take to make the educational system a learning organization – expert at dealing with change as a normal part of its work, not just in relation to the latest policy, but as a way of life." Fullan, M. (1993 p. 4). Change Forces: Probing the Depths of Educational Reform. London: Falmer Press.

"We recommend that schools be restructured to become genuine learning organizations for both students and teachers: organizations that respect learning, honor teaching and teach for understanding" Darling-Hammond, L. (1996 p. 198). What Matters Most: A Competent Teacher for Every Child. Phi Delta Kappan, 78(3), 193-200.

"The framework of a professional learning community is inextricably linked to the effective integration of standards, assessment and accountability... the leaders of professional learning communities balance the desire for professional autonomy with the fundamental principles and values that drive collaboration and mutual accountability." Reeves, D. (2005 pp. 47-48). Putting It All Together: Standards, Assessment, and Accountability in Successful Professional Learning Communities. In R. DuFour, R. Eaker, & R. DuFour (Eds), On Common Ground: The Power of Professional Learning Communities. Bloomington, IN: Solution Tree Press.

"The Use of professional learning communities is the best, least expensive, most professionally rewarding way to improve schools… Such communities hold out immense, unprecedented hope for schools and the improvement of teaching." Schmoker, M. (2005 pp. 137-138). Here and Now: Improving Teaching and Learning. In R. DuFour, R. Eaker & R. DuFour (Eds.), On Common Ground: The Power of Professional Learning Communities. Bloomington IN: Solution Tree Press.

"Well implemented professional learning communities are a powerful means of seamlessly blending teaching and professional learning in ways that produce complex, intelligent behavior in all teachers." Sparks, N. (2005, p.156). Leading for Transformation in Teaching, Learning and Relationships. In R. DuFour, R. Eaker & R. DuFour (Eds.), On Common Ground: The Power of Professional Learning Communities. Bloomington IN: Solution Tree Press.

Organizations Supporting the Effectiveness of Collaboration

"Quality teaching requires strong, professional learning communities. Collegial interchange, not isolation, must become the norm for teachers. Communities of learning can no longer be considered utopian; they must become the building blocks that establish a new foundation for America's schools." National Commission on Teaching and America's Future, (2003, p. 17). No Dream Denied: A Pledge to America's Children. Washington D.C.

"(1) Ensure teachers work interdependently as a professional learning community to guarantee continuous improvement and gains in student achievement.

(2) Create the support and structures necessary to implement a professional learning community.

(3) Ensure a systemic implementation of a professional learning community throughout all aspects of mathematics curriculum, instruction, and assessment at the school, district and regional level." NCTM, (2008). The Prime Leadership Framework: Principles and Indicators for Mathematics Education Leaders. Bloomington IN: Solution Tree Press.

"Effective professional development fosters collegial relationships, creating professional communities where teachers share knowledge and treat each other with respect. Within such communities, teacher inquiry and reflection can flourish and research shows that teachers who engage in collaborative professional development feel confident and well prepared to meet the demands of teaching." NCTE, (2006). NCTE Principles of Adolescent Reform: A Policy Research Brief. Retrieved from http://www.ncte.org/library/files/about_NCTE/Overview/Adol-Lit-Brief.pdf

---

Six keys to a quality school:

1. "The staff has a collective commitment to and takes responsibility for implementing high standards for all students. The school operates under the assumption that all students can learn."
2. "Teachers and staff collaborate to remove barriers to student learning. Teachers communicate regularly with each other about effective teaching and learning strategies."
3. "Student assessment is used for decision making to improve learning. A variety of assessment techniques are used."
4. "Teachers have regularly scheduled time to learn from one another. Professional development has a direct, positive effect on teaching."
5. "Computer hardware and software supplies are adequate for students and teachers. Support services are adequate."
6. "Instruction includes interventions for students who are not succeeding. Teachers are open to new learnings and rethink their approaches to teaching and assessment practices based on teacher-directed action research and other classroom-based inquiries."
   National Education Association, (2003). NEA's School Quality Indicators. Retrieved from:
   http://www/nea.org/schoolquality/index.htm

"Fundamentally reshape school culture, turning the school into a professional learning community, reducing isolation and opening new leadership opportunities for teachers." American Federation of Teachers. (2010). AFT Resolutions: Teacher Development and Evaluation. Retrieved from: http://www/aft.org/about/resolution_detail.cfm?articleid=1548

"Professional learning that increases educator effectiveness and results for all students occurs within learning communities committed to continuous improvement, collective responsibility and goal alignment." Learning Forward (formerly National Staff Development Council). (2011). Standards for Professional Learning: Learning Communities. Retrieved from: http://learning/forward.org/standards/learning-comminities#. UhYXDhYjCwE

Evidence That Collaboration Improves Student Outcomes

Reflection

After reviewing the evidence presented what conclusions do you draw? Do you agree that the evidence is persuasive, that increased educator collaboration contributes significantly to improved student outcomes?

_____

_____

_____

_____

_____

Do you think this evidence would be important to your efforts to improve the collaboration process in your district or school? Why?

_____

_____

_____

_____

_____

Do you think the majority of educators in your district/school would be aware of this body of information?

_____

_____

_____

_____

If they are not particularly aware, do you think it would be important to change their level of awareness? If so, how would you go about that?

_____

_____

_____

_____

_____

Elements Related to Successful
Collaboration Structures

Elements Related to Successful

Collaboration Structures

Most of the researchers, authors, and organizations cited in the previous section have drawn conclusions regarding elements they have found to be associated with more successful collaboration. While there are a number of specific differences in their approach and emphasis there is a remarkable list of similarities. Presented below are descriptions of those elements associated with successful collaboration that appear to cut across many specific school types, levels, content, and organizational schemes. While reviewing these elements one needs to keep in mind that each situation is unique. Context matters and some elements may be more significant or different in one situation than another usually due to the current conditions.

Element (Process/Structural)	Our Current Condition	Strategy to Improve
"Shared vision/common goals" Members of the team have a shared understanding of where they are and where they wish to go. Their vision is clearly stated and goals are clear and measureable.		
"Data/Results oriented" Members are comfortable using data. Opinions are based on data. Evidence is valued over ideology.		

"Structured" The team has enough structure to operate efficiently and effectively but not so much that it is consumed by paperwork and process.		
"Focus on practice/deprivatization" The team uses student data to define the problem and monitor progress, however the team focuses as much or more of their time on their practice, identifying the changes they need to make to change student outcomes and documenting their change in practice.		
"Decision making authority" The parameters of the team's decision-making authority are clear to all parties. Teams are encouraged to advocate for decisions beyond their current scope of authority.		
"Administrative support" Teams have the active support of administration at all levels. Immediate administrators are		

knowledgeable and involved.		
"Adequate/protected time" Teams have adequate time (a minimum of 60 minutes bi-weekly) of time. This time is not interrupted or co-opted for anything else.		
Element (Personal/Emotional)		
"Trust" There is trust between team members. Positions are respected. Decisions are supported. There is trust by the administration for the team to work in the best interests of students		
"Emotional safety" All members of the team can speak freely without fear of being attacked, denigrated or embarrassed. Respectful dialogue. Professional behavior.		
"Collaboration skills" Team members know how to collaborate. They know how to listen actively, clarify, support, and disagree respectively. They are		

sensitive to others feelings but not to the point where disagreements are not allowed to occur.		
"Commitment to the group and the process" Members are not doing this as a compliance exercise. They are not just "going through the motions". Members see the value in the process and want to be successful for the benefit of their students.		
"Growth mindset" Members feel they can grow professionally as a result of the process. Improving instructional skills is important to them and they see this process as a vehicle for professional growth. They associate their professional growth with students' growth.		
"Moral purpose" Members have entered into this process for an underlying higher moral purpose. They embrace the process as an opportunity to change the lives of their students by enhancing their impact.		

"Voluntary, if possible" It is understandable that people will be more likely to enter into a productive collaboration if they have a choice as to whether or not they are going to do it and with whom they collaborate.		

Later in this volume we will be dealing with these issues in more depth.

A Protocol for a Collaborative Team

Protocol for a Collaborative Team

In the pages that follow a protocol for teams of educators working together to solve student performance issues is described. This protocol is described in more detail in "Harnessing the Power of Teacher Teams" published in 2014 by Michael Wasta. This summary is designed to succinctly describe the series of steps a team can take to focus their work on making the necessary changes to their practice in order to create different outcomes for students.

Introduction

This document is designed to be a reference tool for educators involved in the work of a collaborative improvement team. This document can be referred to as the team of educators work their way through the protocol described in the initial training. The document has been created based upon work with dozens of collaborative teams and reflects some of the most common questions and concerns that have arisen.

This document is purposely not designed to be a template that a collaborative team fills in as its work progresses. The emphasis in this process is for a team of educators to think deeply, thoughtfully and collaboratively about their practice and its effect on students, not to spend time filling out forms. The form is a blank piece of paper or a blank computer screen. This protocol is a guide to systematically channel the work of the team. But it is only a guide. If the team finds any part of the protocol to be interfering with its ability to work thoughtfully, deeply and collaboratively the team should modify the protocol to suit its needs.

Finally, this process can be used by any unit in the school district working to implement any initiative. Although we most often think of a group of teachers using this process to improve the effectiveness of their instruction (A Professional Learning Community or Data Team), it can be used by other groups to enhance the implementation of any program or initiative. For example, a superintendent could use the process to have his team implement a new grade structure in the district. Or a curriculum supervisor could use the process to implement a new K-5 math or language arts curriculum. Or a high school science department head could use the process to implement a new approach to laboratory work.

The primary reason for any of these changes should be to improve outcomes for students. By following the data-driven, disciplined implementation steps described in the following document, any collaborative team, implementing any initiative or new program will be forced to hold itself to extremely high standards. As the implementation proceeds the data streams created will constantly inform the implementers about whether or not they are meeting high standards of implementation and whether or not the positive effects on student performance they had anticipated are in fact occurring. Armed with this data the team can make necessary adjustments to their implementation and if necessary abandon the initiative if they cannot produce evidence of its effectiveness.

Part 1

Before we begin we must decide what problem we are trying to solve. Although this might seem obvious, it is interesting how often a school or group of educators invest significant time, energy and funds in a new strategy without first determining what aspect of student performance the strategy is designed to affect.

The simplest way to identify the student performance issue to be addressed is to ask the educators involved. Educators with any experience have a tremendous amount of anecdotal and inferential information concerning the students they serve. It has been this author's experience that educators can readily identify the top three or four student performance issues they encounter on a regular basis.

Step 1. The group of educators involved identifies a significant student performance issue.

Factors to consider when identifying a significant student performance issue:

The issue:

- Should effect a significant number of students
- Should have leverage (if we fix this it will have broad effects)
- Should be seen frequently
- Is agreed upon by the entire team
- May be strictly academic or may be behavioral
- Should not be focused on very discrete academic issues tied to specific instructional units. Since the pace of instruction will move quickly you will not have time to address the issue before moving on.

Process:

- Each educator on the team reflects on the above individually, based upon his/her experience and creates a list of issues
- Educators in the group compare lists and agree on the top 3 or 4 priorities
- The top priority issues are ranked in order
- The issues will be addressed in order

Notes:

This is not usually a difficult step for educators. More difficult is coming to consensus regarding which problem to address.

When starting out it may be preferable for a team to select a more modest issue that will be easier to accomplish. Success in the process initially may be more important that tackling a large/difficult issue.

Comments:

_____

_____

_____

_____

_____

Step 2. Identify a strategy for collecting data regarding the significant student performance issue identified in Step 1.

Although the team relied on educator anecdotal information to develop the significant student performance issue, the team now has to document the issue with data. The team needs to do this for the following reasons:

- Although unlikely, our anecdotal information may be inaccurate. This often occurs with behavioral issues. A few students demonstrating difficult behavior can feel like a much larger number.

- In order to document progress the team needs to establish a starting point or baseline.

The data needed to document the issue may already be available – district tests, unit tests, behavioral records, etc. If the team decides that the available data does an accurate job of describing the current level of student performance, by all means use it.

If, however, the data does not exist, or if the team questions the accuracy of the data, the team will need to identify a data collection strategy. Keep in mind that data collection does not always mean a test. Valuable data can be collected through structured observation, surveys, questionnaires, interviews, etc. Usually if the issue concerns the acquisition of a specific academic skill, some sort of evaluation will be used. If the issue is more behavioral some of the other means listed may be more appropriate. In either case the team needs to decide:

- The vehicle to be used to document the issue
- The schedule and process for data collection

Assuming that the data confirmed our suspicion regarding the significant student performance issue, move on to Step 3. If the data did not confirm our suspicion, move to another issue.

Notes:

Again, this step is usually not difficult for educators. They are used to assessing student performance. If data is available use it. If new data needs to be generated then some assessment scheme needs to be devised. A larger problem is if the data does not support the educators' perception of a problem. There will be a tendency to make the data fit their opinion. The data must objectively support the issue. No data – no issue.

Comments:

_____

_____

_____

_____

_____

Step 3. Create a SMART goal defining the desired student performance level.

Now that the team has documented the student performance issue with data the team can establish a reasonable goal following the SMART goal protocol: S-specific, M-measureable, A-achievable, R-realistic, T-time bound.

Goals and goal setting have become so common that they frequently lose their meaning and impact. Taking the goal setting process seriously requires members of the team to be brutally honest regarding what they feel is possible. Some things to consider when setting the goal:

- How much time will we be able to devote to this issue?
- What additional resources are going to be required?
- How much new learning is going to be required on our part?

It does little good (and perhaps some harm) to set unrealistically high goals only to fail and then have no consequences. This author has witnessed numerous districts and schools in which the repeated practice of setting goals that are never actualized has created an atmosphere of "going through the motions" with no real commitment to doing what will be necessary to achieve the goals. In these schools and districts goal setting has become a hollow, meaningless activity.

Notes:

> *There are two very divergent thoughts about setting goals. One school of thought says the goal should be audacious/grand/big, to serve as an inspiration. The danger to this approach is that as time goes by without achieving the goal people get discouraged. The other thought is that the goal should be modest and achievable in a reasonable period of time. This author recommends that the goal be changeable. Establish a reasonable goal and timeline and when that is achieved, up the goal if necessary.*

Comments:

_____

_____

_____

_____

Step 4. Identify interim data to be used to document student progress.

In the previous step the team determined the ultimate change in behavior it wished to accomplish with the students. This may take some time to achieve. If we don't take frequent data snapshots we may find that we are not making the progress necessary and only find that out when it is too late to make any modifications. The purpose of brief, interim data snapshots is to determine if the strategies we are employing to change student performance appear to be having the desired effect.

The following criteria have been found to be helpful when creating these interim data measures:

- Brief – Remember, this is a snapshot – an assessment that only takes a few minutes to deliver (think quiz not test).
- Frequent – approximately once every week or two, depending on the issue.
- Common to all educators on the team.

Process:

- Establish the schedule and stick to it unless the team decides to change.
- Share construction of the actual assessments.
- Bring scored assessments to scheduled meetings.
- Graph data and discuss.
- Questions – Was it a good assessment? What does the data say about progress? How does the data correlate with the data about change in practice?

Notes:

> *This is a critical step. What the team is actually constructing at this point is a series of common formative assessments (CFA's). CFA's have been shown to be a powerful agent in improving outcomes for students. This has proven to be a difficult step for many teams.*
>
> *Constructing and administering these assessments calls for teachers to surrender some of their autonomy. Usually the design of quizzes (to use a dated term) is the sole prerogative of an individual teacher. Don't underestimate the difficulty some teachers*

will have in giving up this autonomy. Also, making the results public with the inevitable differences in scores is a significant issue for many teachers. Although the differences in student performance offer a tremendous opportunity for meaningful collaboration for teachers by asking the more successful teacher, "What did you do to get those results?", the fear of "deprivatization" of practice at this point frequently rears its head.

Comments:

_____

_____
_____
_____
_____
_____
_____
_____

Part 2

It is at this point that this protocol begins to differ from many other collaborative protocols (Data Teams, PLC's). In Part 1 the team did a rigorous, thorough job of identifying and documenting the student performance issue of concern. Now the team will enter into an equally rigorous, thorough job of determining what they as professionals are going to change in order to change the arc of student performance with which they are dissatisfied.

Step 5. The educators involved identify that aspect of their practice that will have to be changed if they are to positively influence student performance.

Part A.

The group of educators involved will have to accept the notion that what they have been doing is not getting the results they desire. We know that other variables beyond the educators' control are often influencing the situation (home support, student attitudes and abilities for example). But we also know that the actions educators take also influence the situation – A LOT! So if we are to move in a positive direction over which we have control, at this point the team is going to take an honest, brutal, factual look at their current practice(s) with the aim of discovering what they can do more of, less of, and/or differently to influence the students' performance in the direction we desire. The team's focus needs to remain primarily on changes they will need to make. Although the team may identify changes others need to make, that will not be the primary focus of our effort.

Similar to the guidelines used in the student performance phase, the actions the team decides to focus upon should meet the following criteria:

- Have leverage. If we change this, we will likely get a big effect with regard to the student performance issue
- Involve reasonable, realistic, attainable actions
- Focus primarily on actions members of the team will take

Process:

A way to get started is to have each member of the team describe in detail how he/she has been addressing the student performance issue individually.

Members of the team may each conduct individual research about alternative ways the issue has been addressed by others.

The team may need to seek out people with expertise and knowledge.

This step may take some time. Take the time. A great deal of time and energy is going to be spent learning about and implementing whatever is chosen. Making the best choice at the outset will save time in the long run. Similarly to the thought and care the team invested in identifying the student performance issue, the team must be even more thoughtful regarding the proposed solution upon which they are about to embark in hopes of solving the problem.

A general guideline should be that there is a consensus on the team that this strategy, procedure, plan or practice, if implemented well, stands a reasonable chance of significantly improving the identified student issue.

Notes:

Arguably this is one of the most important steps in the process. This is where real educator learning begins to take place. Please refer to the article by Reeves and DuFour titled, "PLC Light" in Appendix A. Making the shift from a focus on the students to a focus on themselves is a game changer for teachers. All of the issues about private practice and being threatened are likely to surface to some degree. Reassurance may be needed. Teachers have frequently not been asked to find such answers themselves. Also, most systems do not allow enough space and time for teachers to do a good job at this. When it is communicated to teachers that there is no rush; that this should be a careful, thoughtful, professional exploration of possibilities, they frequently don't really believe that. The actions of the leader here are critical. Patience and encouragement need to be the by-words.

Sometimes the solution the team decides upon is quite frankly, terrible, unrealistic, unlikely to succeed, etc. One way to help avoid this possibility is to establish Consideration Standards in advance. These are a simple list of criteria any proposed action must contain. For example: Evidence that this action has solved the problem in a similar situation, is reasonable in terms of cost, and can be implemented in a reasonable period of time.

Comments:

_____

_____

_____

_____

_____

Step 5.

Part B.

After identifying the strategy, practice, procedure, or structure needed to improve student performance in general the team needs to become more specific. Therefore the team will move on to describe what the new practice or strategy will look like if it is implemented at an exemplary level. After all, why would the team strive to be fair or mediocre implementers? The standard must be exemplary.

When we fail to articulate the specific characteristics of a practice or strategy, the danger is that different implementers will form their own, often very different ideas of what implementation should look like – all thinking that they are doing what they should be doing even when objective measurement would illuminate vast differences. In such situations, *the team may then conclude the new strategy or procedure isn't effective, when in fact, it was the inconsistent, low level of implementation that was the problem.*

This very common problem can be avoided if the team creates a set of observable/measureable standards for exemplary implementation.

Process:

- As a team, create a vision or image of what exemplary implementation of the practice would look like.
- Identify a limited number of essential elements of exemplary implementation. An element is essential if its absence means the implementation is not exemplary.
- Describe these essential elements specifically enough that a casual observer could determine if they are present or not.

By the end of this process, the team has created a crisp, clear set of standards defining what exemplary implementation of their practice should look like. And by limiting this definition to only the essential standards the team has allowed for differentiation as to exactly how those essential elements are presented by each teacher. By focusing on essential elements, the team can allow for individual teacher creativity in how the element is presented and at the same time have each member of the team be held accountable for ensuring that each essential element is addressed.

Notes:

> *This is another critical, difficult step. Based upon years and years of practice educators of all types are prone to describe a practice in vague, general terms. One suspects that this lack of clarity and specificity is related to the issue of "Teacher as Artisan". The notion that each individual teacher must be free to design the strategy as he/she likes based upon the unique circumstances of his/her classroom. Equally operational here is the American idea of independence. Conforming to a strict set of procedures really rankles many teachers. "I don't need to read from a script". Some notable scripted programs have left a definite "bad taste" in many teachers' minds. There can be common ground here. By identifying a limited number (5-8) of essential elements of a strategy the group can strive for a common understanding of what the strategy should look like if implemented well while at the same time not tying a teacher's hands completely. The way an individual teacher implements an essential element may be very idiosyncratic while still maintaining the integrity of the element. Presenting the group with several examples here is usually helpful. In the end, it has been found to be critical that every person to whom the standards are going to be applied have the opportunity to comment on each standard. Again, patience and persistence will likely be necessary. See "Squeezing the Accordion" in Appendix E. See article, "Words Matter", by Eermeling, Ermeling & Gallimore in Appendix C and "PLC's on Steroids" by this author in Appendix B.*

Comments:

_____
_____
_____
_____
_____
_____

Step 6. Document each member of the teams' current level of implementation of the new practice, procedure or strategy.

Just as with the student data, the team needs to create a baseline of current implementation. The two most common ways to collect this data are peer observation or video. In either case, by viewing the practice and comparing what is observed to the essential element standards described in the previous step the team can determine each member's current level of implementation. Remember, if **any** essential element is missing, the exemplary standard is not met.

If the team takes the baseline measure (the metric is % of observed practice meeting **all** standards) and finds that our implementation is already very high (85-100%), then we have probably chosen the wrong practice. After all, if we are already doing this well and are still getting poor student results, we probably need to look elsewhere.

The bottom line is that a low implementation number at this point indicates that we have uncovered a high leverage practice that we are currently not implementing very well. Thus, we can be hopeful that as our implementation improves, so will the impact on student performance. **If we have chosen a new, complex practice** *a baseline score of 0% exemplary implementation would not be surprising and in many ways would be good news.*

Notes:

Again, we are heading into very new territory for most teachers. In the past most observations of teacher's practice has been for evaluation purposes. That is not what is happening here. To emphasize that point the author recommends that no administrator be involved in collecting this data and that the issue be separate from whatever evaluation scheme is present in the school. We are asking teachers to let others see them performing at less than their best. A scary proposition for anyone! Having tried a number of approaches to this issue this author recommends that video be used. Several schools have successfully had teacher's video a slice of their own instruction around the strategy of concern (using their own cell phone or iPad) and at their convenience review the video and look for the absence or presence of each of the essential elements identified by the team. In this author's experience teachers have been very honest in this process. No teacher needs to share his/her video if he/she does not wish to do so. A note of caution here: Teacher's recollection of how they did in implementing the strategy without evidence such as video is likely to be inaccurate. Evidence exists that teachers need structure to accurately recall their implementation of a strategy. Absent such structure they are likely to overstate their implementation. See the article," Accuracy of Teacher Reports of Their Classroom Behavior" by Hook & Rosenshine in Appendix D.

Especially in the early stages teachers' scores should be anonymous: Teacher A, B, C etc.

Some teachers may now begin to argue that some element is not really essential (particularly if they didn't include it). This why it is important for everyone to have had an opportunity to determine the essential elements. No element can be changed unilaterally by any teacher. The group decision can be revisited, but <u>only the team can change the essential elements</u>. This is where collaborative practice and private practice meet head on. If an individual teacher balks at this point this is a serious issue. It must be resolved to preserve the integrity of the process. The best way is for the team, not the administrator to deal with the issue. Fortunately this situation is not common. The power of the group can be very beneficial here. In the rare case of an individual who will just not conform, and will not respond to the team the team may have to recommend that the person be removed.

Comments:

_____

_____

_____

_____

_____

_____

_____

Step 7. Create a SMART goal defining desired teacher behavior.

Just as the team did with the student issue, the team now creates a SMART goal that articulates the change in educators' behavior concerning the chosen practice.

If we assume the level of exemplary implementation was at 0% when the baseline was taken the SMART goal may look like:

"By June 2016 the % of exemplary implementation of XYZ practice will increase from 0 in September 2015 to 90% as measured by the Standards for Exemplary Implementation created by the team."

Notes:

This goal must be set very high. Research by Dr. Douglas Reeves (Reeves, 2006) has found that for a practice to have dramatic impact on student performance it must be implemented at a very high rate*. His research has found that the relationship between implementation of a strategy and student performance is not linear. In other words, going from 10% exemplary implementation to 50% exemplary implementation will not result in student performance improving by a corresponding 40%. It is only when exemplary implementation reaches 85 to 90% that we then see a dramatic spike in student performance. This finding makes the next step, collecting interim data regarding implementation so important.

Reeves, D. (2006). The Learning Leader . Alexandra, VA: Association for Supervision and Curriculum Development

Comments:

_____

_____

_____

_____

_____

_____

_____

_____

_____

_____

_____

_____

Step 8. Identify interim data to be used to document educator progress.

As with the student data, the team cannot wait an entire year to determine if progress has been made. Therefore the team needs to identify what data will be collected on an interim basis. Usually this data takes the form of periodic observations or video clips to which the implementation standards are applied.

Frequently as this process unfolds the team will identify those elements that are being implemented at a high level and some elements that are proving problematic. This data allows the team to focus its learning energy on the troublesome elements.

Again, the data must be collected frequently enough to inform the team and its' actions. A brief observation or video clip collected every 3 to 4 weeks is usually sufficient. Frequency however is determined by how quickly the team feels changes are being made.

The process used by the team follows the same guidelines as those for collecting student data.

Notes:

This is frequently another very new area for educators. But it is critical. The data that is collected will guide the work the team does. For example if the team finds that certain elements are proving more difficult than others they can focus their learning there. This data also allow the team to differentiate for individual members. This practice, while critically important, can be extremely difficult for educators who have been in an environment where everyone has been critically important, can be extremely difficult for educators who have been in an environment where everyone has been considered equal. (The Lake Woebegone Effect). The fact is that people learn things at different rates. Acknowledging this and providing differentiated support is one of the strengths of this approach. This avoids the "one size fits all" professional development frequently disparaged by teachers. For the leader, playing the role of "Minimal Mike" has been found to relieve some of the stress at this point. Minimal Mike is described as the weakest member of the team who will only rise to the lowest level of performance. For example if the team decided to focus on quality feedback and does not describe this in any detail, Mike will tell his students, "You all did great!" and really feel he implemented the strategy. Also as individual "high flyers" are identified they can be an invaluable resource for everyone else. Once again the team will have to get past the issue of no one standing out against others. Everyone knows it but no one talks openly about it. Patience and encouragement is critical here. Pushing too hard could be disastrous.

Comments:

_____

_____

_____

_____

_____

_____

Step 9. Describe the process to be used to change teacher behavior.

In previous protocols the direction was for the team to write out a plan of action covering all of the steps the team was going to take over an extended period of time. In reality such a process makes little sense. The team is now entering an extended collaborative learning process. Exactly where this process is going to take the team is almost always unknown. Therefore what is suggested in this step is that the team records its progress over time. Documentation of the actions of the team is important but this documentation cannot be anticipated (See Dynamic Planning).

Process:

- Team members must determine where they are going to start their learning process.
- Frequently the baseline data will illuminate a teacher or two who is well ahead of the others in the process. Observation, video study of these teachers is a good first step.
- Share specific instructional ideas in team meetings, where each member is charged with bringing one good idea to a meeting.

- Collect and observe on-line and professionally produced video of implementation of the practice.
- Recruit experts within the school or district to come to team meetings.
- Teachers can practice the new idea in a team meeting with peers serving as students.
- As these and similar actions are taken by the team, a member of the team serves as the recorder of what is discussed at each team meeting and what was decided. These brief summary notes are distributed to all team members. (People are busy and will forget otherwise.) It is recommended that this information be recorded electronically on a shared site. Don't be lengthy here. Usually completing the following phrases will suffice: "Today we discussed…" and "Today we decided…" and "Next steps…"

Notes:

Since this level of control of what they are going to learn and how they are going to learn it is new to many teams, patience is needed. The administrator should refrain from telling the team what to do at this point. Some "productive struggle" may be appropriate here. This is the team's learning and should be decided by the team. If a couple of meetings are spent with false starts it is a small price to pay for the team to take serious ownership of the process. Trust these professionals to find the way. After all they are all professional educators.

It is crucial that a record of the actions of the team be kept. At the same time this record should be succinct. A half or three quarter pages summary done at the meeting by the recorder electronically and distributed immediately is usually sufficient.

Comments:

_____
_____
_____
_____
_____
_____

Step 10. Compare educator data changes to student data changes.

Part of the on-going work of the team is to monitor two data streams - student and educator. When the educators feel they have made some significant changes to their practice as documented with their interim data, they may wish to schedule a snapshot of student data. A word of caution here: **Remember, *Dr. Reeves' research has found that the implementation often has to reach the 90% level before dramatic changes in student outcome become apparent.*** Because of this delayed effect, many teachers give up on a strategy just before it is about to create the desired student effect.

The correlation between the two sets of data can guide the team's decision-making process. As they see practice improve, especially when it approaches the 90% implementation level they should be seeing corresponding changes in student outcomes. If not, the team has to make a critical decision. How long do we continue our course before we change? There are no prepackaged answers to this question. The team will have to make the most professional judgment they can, based upon the data.

The good news however is that this is rare. If the team has followed a thoughtful, flexible process to this point almost always there is a significant change in student outcomes.

Notes:

It is critical that the team continue the process until the student performance issue is solved. In the research cited at the beginning of the process, it was found that when collaborative teacher teams actually saw that their enhanced/changed/improved practice resulted in improved outcomes for students, the teams became powerfully successful. This research even found that there appeared to be a generalized improvement in teacher's effectiveness in areas not under team scrutiny.

In the examples of Dynamic Planning presented later one can see how teams navigate their way to greater learning and implementation. At least initially this may be slow with a number of false starts. The team that struggles through this frustrating phase will be amply rewarded for its persistence.

Comments:

_____

_____

_____

_____

_____

_____

When the data concerning student performance reaches a level that has been identified in the SMART goal or when the data concerning educator practice reaches the level identified in the practice SMART goal the team has to make a decision. If both SMART goals are realized it is time for the team to begin the process anew with a new area of student performance as the focus. If the educator practice SMART goal is realized but the student goal has yet to be reached it is likely that the practice the team focused on is not, by itself, powerful enough to move student performance to the desired level. In such cases the team needs to return to step 5 to consider what needs to be added to their practice. Does a new practice need to be developed? Or does the current level of implementation of the practice need to be raised? These are difficult questions that will require a thoughtful, professional approach by the team.

In either case, the work of the team never ends. This is an iterative process designed to seek constant improvement and refinement of practice in service to the needs of the students.

Dynamic Improvement Planning

Formal school improvement planning has become commonplace in public education. These plans frequently follow a structured process that includes a description of current student performance, establishment of measureable goals and the construction of an action plan describing all of the steps the school will take to move from its present level of student performance to the desired performance described in the goals. This list of actions is often lengthy and articulate actions the adults will take to change the performance of students. These plans are typically constructed at the beginning of each school year, implemented during the school year and evaluated at the end of the school year. The entire process is usually managed by a team of professionals in the school led by the principal. The process is repeated the following year and the following year, etc. By faithfully implementing these plans some schools have been able to make demonstrable improvement in student performance some of the time. However, many schools have yet to realize such improvement.

There are four major flaws in many of these plans. The first flaw involves attempting to identify all of the actions the adults will need to take throughout the year even before the year has begun. The second flaw involves describing these actions in vague, un-measureable terms. The third flaw is making unrealistic assumptions concerning the time and effort that will be required to achieve a significant change in adult behaviors. And finally, the last flaw concerns putting far more in the plan than can possibly be accomplished. By limiting the focus to fewer goals, the likelihood of meeting success rises. By moving from this static, prescribed format to a more dynamic, long-term, flexible, real-time format, schools can address these flaws and improve the effectiveness of this process. In this dynamic process the school team charged with designing and implementing the plan will begin in the same manner; by identifying those student performance issues of greatest concern. Data is collected to describe students' historic and current level of performance; goals for improved performance are established and assessment schemes for measuring progress are designed. However, when it comes to identifying what changes in adult behavior need to take place to change the level of student performance identified, the team does not attempt to identify all of the steps in the process that will be necessary. The problem with that approach is that the school team rarely can anticipate the course such a plan needs to take with any degree of accuracy. And by guessing (literally) at all of the actions that will occur over the course of the year and the sequence in which they will occur, the team will frequently end up doing things that no longer are appropriate, simply because they are in the plan.

By contrast, in dynamic planning the team only writes the plan to a point where data may require a change in direction. For example:

An elementary school has determined that many students are not making adequate progress in the acquisition of mathematics knowledge. They are particularly concerned about the students' performance on the new State assessment. With assistance from district personnel, the school has learned that if students engage in high quality peer discourse about mathematical ideas on a regular basis they are likely to improve their performance. Through its own research the school defines what high quality student discourse looks like in practice and by conducting structured observations of students engaging in discourse determines that their students are not engaging in high quality peer discourse with sufficient frequency to improve mathematics performance. They have data documenting the students' current level of performance and have established a goal for improvement. As the team begins to think about how teacher behavior will have to change in order to bring about this change in student discourse they discover that they do not have sufficient knowledge about what best practice in this area actually looks like in the classroom. They determine that the first step in their action plan is to educate themselves about this topic. They create assignments for various members in order to gather this information including, literature searches, contact with district and/or state department of education resources, and perhaps university resources. They establish a tentative date by which all of this information will be collected and brought back to the team.

At this point this team cannot reasonably anticipate what will happen after the information is shared. They may conclude that more information is needed prior to moving forward. They may even decide that based upon what they discovered, they will pursue another avenue. If the entire plan had been written out the team may move in a direction that no longer makes sense based upon their expanded knowledge. In static plans this is frequently exactly what happens.

Returning to our example, let us assume that the team is satisfied with its research and is able to articulate a limited number of essential characteristics of teacher practice that appear to be correlated with improved student peer discourse. Before rushing to implement professional development about this topic, the team decided they needed to ascertain teachers' current level of implementation. After all, perhaps some or even many of the teachers are already employing the practices they have uncovered. The team decides to collect video snapshots of teacher's practice and score each against the essential characteristics they have determined define exemplary practice in this area. They establish a date by which all of this data will be submitted to the team.

Here again, the team cannot describe what actions will be taken until they review the data. The proper course would be radically different if the data indicates a high percentage of the staff is already meeting the exemplary level of implementation vs. few or none. Therefore, it is again prudent for the team to review the data before determining the next step.

Returning to our example, let's assume the data revealed that 90% of the staff was meeting less than half of the 6 essential characteristics they had identified as defining exemplary practice. This is actually good news since the team has identified a potentially powerful practice that they now know they are not implementing very well. Therefore, they have reason to believe that if they improve their implementation it will have a significant effect on student performance. The team has also learned something else. A few of the teachers are already quite proficient in the practice and can serve as a valuable resource.

Armed with this information the team can now articulate the actions they will take to raise the level of implementation for the staff. Using the information from their original research, the data from their overall current level of implementation and most importantly, the expertise of the few good implementers the team determines that they will construct a fairly traditional workshop session to present all of this information to the entire staff. A date is set for the workshop. The team also persuades the good implementers to allow video of their work to be shared with all staff in a follow-up to the general workshop. A date is scheduled for this session.

Once again, the team cannot reasonably anticipate what course the plan will take following these two steps. While educators talk incessantly about differentiating instruction for students, this is rarely done when we consider adult learning. In our example isn't it likely that the change in implementation following these two workshops will vary considerably from teacher to teacher? Assuming all staff will implement any practice at an exemplary level on a universal timeline is one of the greatest errors teams frequently make.

In this case our hypothetical team decides they will take another video snapshot of the practice following both workshops. What the team will do then will be determined entirely by the data. Let's look at some of the possibilities:

1. The data is essentially unchanged from the previous measure.
2. The vast majority of teachers are now meeting the standards of exemplary implementation.
3. Most of the teachers have improved but some have not.
4. Some of the teachers have improved but most have not.

Wouldn't the proper course of action at this point be drastically different based upon which description above applies?

Again, if the team had made assumptions about all of this and laid out and followed a plan with all steps predetermined they could be moving much too quickly for the staff or moving much to slowly and forcing people into training they could be giving!

Returning one more time to our example, let's assume the data indicated that some of the staff (20%) had improved their implementation significantly (meeting 75% of the criteria) but most (65%) had not. In this case our team decided they needed to understand why the 2 workshops had such minimal effect on 65% of the staff. Therefore they will conduct focused interviews with some of this group while conducting a survey of all members. Simultaneously they will ask their good implementers to provide some one-on-one coaching to those staff members who did make significant changes – differentiation! And so the process continues and evolves.

By now it should be apparent that in a dynamic improvement process, the plan never ends, it continuously evolves, informed both by data concerning student performance as well as data concerning changes in adult behavior.

It will also be apparent to many that there are a number of structural and cultural impediments present in many schools that will make implementation of such a model difficult if not impossible. Some of these impediments are:

1. From the example above it is obvious that a process like the one described takes a great deal of time. Many schools find that they simply cannot create enough time for teachers to work in a collaborative manner to the extent necessary to do this thoughtful work. Time is a factor in another way as well.

Traditional plans are often expected to be carried out over a relatively brief timeline. In fact, if teachers are to effect a significant change in their practice it may take them a long time. This additional time for collaboration is created in many ways in schools; using substitutes to cover teachers classes, paying teachers to extend their day in the morning or afternoon, rearranging the school schedule to release groups of teachers, and renegotiating contracts to increase the teacher day beyond that of the students to name a few.

2. In many districts and schools this level of program design and decision-making is not something to be entrusted to schools and teachers. In these systems, all decisions as to what teachers need to learn and how they need to learn it are made by administrators, district staff and/or a district committee composed of administrators and teachers. This top-down design for teacher learning is quite common. In contrast, in the model described earlier there was a role for district staff in identifying a potentially powerful practice but the implementation was left to the teachers in a school.

3. These plans are "messy". In dynamic planning the plan is always under construction. As such it is difficult for many administrators (district and school) to abandon the tidy plan that can be bound and copied and achieved (and put on a shelf). Dynamic planning is most effectively constructed and documented electronically. By using programs such a "Google docs" the team can create the plan in a continuous file that is shared with all staff and the district on a continuous basis.

Implementing a dynamic planning process in the manner described above also addresses the other three common flaws in the traditional process- the lack of measureable data concerning changes in adult behavior, unrealistic expectations concerning how long changing adult behavior will take and putting too much in the plan.

Schools and districts frequently significantly underestimate the length of time teachers need to master a new or enhanced strategy to the point that they can implement that strategy at a high level in their classrooms. We know that teachers usually need multiple opportunities to try a new strategy in the context of their individual classrooms before they can implement the strategy in a smooth almost automatic manner. In spite of this knowledge, district and school leaders still consider the issue resolved when the scheduled Professional Development (PD) session is completed. In reality, the process is just beginning when the PD session is completed.

The second deficiency this process addresses is the almost complete absence of data concerning teacher implementation of the strategy. The question is not, is the teacher implementing the strategy? Rather the question should be is the teacher implementing the strategy well? All too often the school and or district have no data on the number of teachers implementing the strategy at a defined level. Following the PD there is usually an assumption that all teachers are implementing the strategy at a high level. On the face of it this is an unrealistic assumption. By creating data on teacher implementation the team can differentiate the support teachers need to reach high levels of implementation.

The final common problem this process can address is the issue of multiple initiatives. In an effort to address all problems simultaneously, districts and schools layer initiative after initiative upon their teachers. This layering virtually insures shallow learning and implementation, as teachers attempt to address the new math program, the new literacy program and the new behavior program, etc. simultaneously. As one can see by the depth and breadth of work described in the example above, in most schools there is simply not enough time to do this process well with more than one initiative at a time. There is also some evidence to suggest that allowing teachers to focus deeply on one initiative and bringing about improved student performance in that area as a result of improved practice on the part of the teachers brings about a generalized improvement in all of their practice even in areas not specifically addressed! (McDougall, Saunders, & Goldenberg 2007).

As you look at the two examples of School Improvement Planning below, ask yourself which plan reflects what is actually happening in the school. In the traditional model how could the authors of this plan possibly know what would be the appropriate course of action to take 6 to 8 months in advance? The first action demonstrates a very common problem. The statement seems to indicate that the school wishes to develop a "shared understanding of the Response To Intervention (RTI) process". The way they will accomplish this apparently is to attend a district professional development activity and hold a staff meeting. There is no attempt to actually articulate a shared understanding and certainly no measure to indicate that this was accomplished. So often going to the professional development is seen as accomplishing the goal. In reality, the professional development activity is the beginning of the process, not the end. It is unrealistic to think that having attended the same professional development activity, all staff will have an equally deep understanding of the process. Unfortunately this is all too common.

In contrast, in the dynamic planning process, this team will have real evidence that they have developed a deep shared understanding of what high quality student performance looks like in the classroom and later evidence as to what exemplary teacher action looks like.

Traditional School Improvement Planning	Dynamic School Improvement Planning
Student Performance Data is Identical	Student Performance Data is Identical
Action Plan	Action Plan

This entire plan was written in August of 2015.*	9/2/15- The team decided that they needed to improve the Response to Intervention (RTI) process in their school. This decision was reached after the team compared their current process to the Standards for Exemplary RTI document. This information indicated that their school RTI process was deficient in 8 of the 10 areas listed. The goal became: "By June 2016 the RTI process at X school will meet exemplary status in 10 of 10 areas as measured by the Standards for Exemplary RTI document."
Develop a shared understanding of the Response to Intervention (RTI) process. District PD 8/15, Staff meeting 10/15, On-going	
Notify parents of their role in the process and modify District letters to ensure parents are viewed as members of the team. 12/15.	
Ensure student SMART goals are being written to ensure long-range success in literacy and numeracy. 12/1/15 and on going.	9/15/15 - The team decided that the entire staff needed to have a much deeper understanding of the components of an exemplary
Ensure progress monitoring is taking place, as it is determined during the goal	

setting process. On-going.

Provide professional development as we encounter areas of teacher weakness within the intervention or enrichment process. On-going.

This is the material that the school provided to document its progress.

(Yes, you're correct. There was no documentation of progress. The plan was filed and forgotten.)

*Taken from an actual school improvement plan.

RTI process. Therefore the Director of Instruction for the District who is an acknowledged expert on this topic will hold a whole staff workshop on 10/6/15.

10/10/15 – Based upon feedback from the PD the staff is concerned that they will have to make a great deal of change to create an exemplary RTI process in our school. Given our current workload we are concerned where the time will come from to undertake such a huge initiative. We are considering a multi-year learning process. A draft of this process with a timeline will be sent to all staff for comment. We will review the results at our next meeting.

10/26/15 – Results of the timeline review finds the vast majority of staff feeling that the timeline is realistic (3 years) and worth pursuing. We will begin with addressing the quality of Tier 1 Instruction…

Dynamic school improvement planning is not a 'silver bullet". It will not solve all of the problems in a school. What it will do is allow a school to plan for improving significant aspects of its work in a deep and meaningful manner. It will allow a school to develop evidence of changes in practice and the relationship of those changes to student performance. It will move the school improvement process from one largely focused on form and transform it into a process focused on substance--results.

McDougall, D., Saunders, W.M., Goldenberg, C. (2007). Inside the Black Box of School Reform: Explaining the how and why of change at Getting Results Schools. International Journal of Disability, Development and Education. 54 (1), 51-86.

Dynamic Planning Examples

Secondary School

8/20/16

The English Department Data Team met to brainstorm the most significant student performance issue presently facing our department. We narrowed the list to the following:

1. The overall performance of ELL students.
2. The quantity and quality of homework completion in general.
3. The ability of students to demonstrate exemplary performance when it comes to tasks requiring higher order thinking skills.

At the conclusion of the meeting three subgroups were formed to gather additional information about each issue and report their findings at the next meeting on 9/7/16.

9/7/16

Following a lively discussion the team decided that issue #3 would be our focus. This decision was made for the following reasons – it affected the greatest number of students, it aligns well with the new CCSS and State assessment and it is important for post-high school success.

The team decided that none of the currently collected data met our needs in this area. Therefore we decided to collect our own data. A subcommittee composed of Bryan, Ann and Barry volunteered to research and produce a common understanding of what we mean by higher order thinking skills and present this to the team at our next meeting on 9/23/16.

9/23/16

We could not agree on a common understanding and agreed to continue the dialogue at our next meeting on 9/30/16.

9/30/16

The team agreed on a common understanding (see document) and asked each course to design one assessment designed to measure student

---

performance in this area by 10/15/16.

10/15/16

Assessments were shared. As a result of this collaboration several assessments were tweaked. It was agreed that all assessments would be administered by 11/1/16 and data reported in a common format for our meeting on 11/18/16.

11/18/16

At our meeting the following data was reported:

Percent of Students Performing at Exemplary Level	
Course	Percent
English I	28
English 2	17
British Writers	26
AP English	49
Overall Average	31

The team concluded that the data confirmed our feeling that students at all levels were not currently producing the sophistication of thinking we had identified as important. The team constructed the following student SMART goal:

"By June, 2017 the percentage of students performing at the exemplary level on the higher-order thinking assessment will increase from 31% to 45% and by at least 10% in each course."

12/3/16

The team began a discussion on instructional practices we would need to consider changing in order to assist the students meet the SMART goal we had crafted. We will continue this discussion at our next meeting on

12/17/16 with the hope of narrowing our focus.

12/17/16

The team decided to focus on three practice areas – Questioning strategies, Transfer of agency strategies, and Performance activity strategies. Each member of the department will join a team of their choice to research and learn about one of these strategies. We developed the following tentative Practice SMART goal:

"By April 2017, the English Department Data Team will identify exemplary practice in the following areas of practice designed to elicit higher-order thinking from students – questioning, transfer of agency and performance tasks as measured by standards created for the purpose."

1/4/17

Each subcommittee is underway and reported to the English Department Data Team. The Questioning strategy subcommittee is struggling with coming to consensus regarding "best practice". Bryan the Department chair will meet with the groups to assist. All subcommittees hope to have identified essential components of best practice in their area by the end of January.

1/18/17

The transfer of agency subcommittee presented their concept of best practice outlining 6 essential components of any activity meeting exemplary level in this area. The performance task subcommittee is well on its way to identifying essential components and hopes to finish by the end of the month. The questioning subcommittee is still struggling. They simply cannot seem to come to consensus regarding what exemplary questioning looks like. The team decided to reach out to the district to request outside assistance.

1/30/17

The transfer of agency subcommittee and performance task subcommittee have both completed work on the first draft of exemplary practice and will be taking baseline data next week. The questioning committee is scheduled to meet with a professor from the University who is an expert in this area next week to attempt to get back on track.

2/12/17

Baseline data from the transfer of agency subcommittee indicates that 25% of observed lessons met all of the exemplary criteria. The performance task subcommittee indicates that 31% of observed tasks met all of the exemplary criteria. Both subcommittees however identified superior performers. People will be freed to observe these classes and they will ask these superior performers to present at their meetings. The questioning committee had a great meeting with Professor Marks and feel they are finally in agreement.

3/1/17

New data from the transfer of agency and performance task subcommittees finds the average of exemplary implementation has jumped from 25% to 42% and 31% to 57% respectively Both groups plan on taking student data next week. Questioning subcommittee has identified essential elements and is completing clear standards of implementation. The team discussed holding a English Department Practice Fair at the end of the year to share our work across the department. Chairman Bryan will work on this.

3/15/17

Student data from the transfer of agency subcommittee finds students performing at the exemplary level on higher-order thinking tasks moved from 28% to 35% in those classes implementing transfer of agency strategies. Performance task classes moved from an average of 19% to 27%. Baseline data on practice for the questioning committee will take place next week.

4/2/17

Practice data from transfer of agency subcommittee moved up to 68% exemplary and performance task practice data moved up to 75% exemplary. Baseline for questioning was at 59% exemplary.

4/18/17

Student data has increased in all classes on higher-order thinking skills demonstration. The department wide average is now up to 48% exemplary! Bryan reports that the Department Practice Fair is scheduled for the day after school gets out on June 17th. Each subcommittee should be prepared to make a data rich presentation to members outside of their committee. The idea is to have everyone increase their awareness and ability to implement best practice in each area.

5/1/17

Exemplary implementation levels have increased again! Performance task is now at 80%, transfer of agency is at 70% and questioning is at 65%. We have wildly exceeded our goal. We decided to include a celebration aspect into the Department Practice Fair in June.

5/18/17

Our most recent snapshot of student data reveals the following:

Percent of Students Performing at Exemplary Level	
Course	Percent
English I	From 28 to 39%
English 2	From 17 to 48%
British Writers	From 26 to 44%
AP English	From 49 to 56%
Overall Average	From 31 to 52%

This is tremendous growth. We anticipate that when all three strategies are spread across all classes we will see student performance grow even more.

8/25/15

The School Data Team identified the declining performance of exiting kindergarten student's acquisition of phonemic awareness (PA) skills as a significant student performance issue and has charged our Kindergarten Data Team with identifying solutions. The School Team cited the following data to document this problem:

May Phonemic Awareness Assessment

2012 - % scoring at/above exemplary level -------------------------- 80%

2013 -% scoring at/above exemplary level -------------------------- 72%

2014- -% scoring at/above exemplary level -------------------------- 70%

2015--% scoring at/above exemplary level -------------------------- 65%

In addition the school team noted that Readiness screening results on these students in the fall of each year have shown similar declines.

Fall Reading Readiness Assessment

2012 - % above benchmark ---------75%

2013 - % above benchmark ---------70%

2014 - % above benchmark ---------68%

The School Data Team has suggested the following SMART goal regarding student performance:

"The % of students scoring at the exemplary level on the May PA assessment will increase from 65% in Spring of 2015 to 85% by Spring 2016."

At our meeting today the Kindergarten team decided to explore this issue in depth to attempt to determine why these scores are dropping so dramatically. Everyone will think about this and review this data and come to our next meeting prepared to suggest a plan of action.

9/12/15

The consensus among members of the kindergarten team is that our current phonemic awareness program is not powerful enough to meet the needs of our more challenged student population. Team member Meagan presented the following information which seems to confirm this point:

Student Performance on the Fall Reading Readiness measure correlated with performance on the Spring Phonemic Awareness Assessment;

Students scoring below benchmark on the Fall Readiness Assessment scored 48% at exemplary on the Spring Phonemic Awareness Assessment.

Students scoring above benchmark on the Fall Reading Readiness Assessment scored at 86% at exemplary on the Spring Phonemic Awareness Assessment.

This data would indicate that students who arrive at kindergarten less prepared are not acquiring the PA skills at a rate anywhere near the more ready student using the same PA program.

The team concluded that they needed to look for ways to strengthen the existing PA program.

We wrote the following interim Teacher Practice SMART goal:

"By January 2017 the kindergarten team will identify and implement a revised PA Awareness Training designed to take 85% of students who scored below the Readiness benchmark in the Fall to the exemplary level on the Spring PA assessment."

All members are asked to think about this goal and bring suggestions to our next meeting as to how we should proceed to realize the goal.

9/30/15

Many excellent suggestions were brought to the meeting and discussed. The team decided that we needed to determine if the problem is our current PA program as described or our IMPLEMENTATION of the current program. Therefore it was decided that each kindergarten teacher will keep a detailed journal of their implementation of the current PA program for two weeks. In addition, each teacher will be given a copy of the book," Developing Phonemic Awareness in Children" to read. At our next meeting we will review the journals and begin discussing the first section of the book.

10/9/15

Review of the journals revealed a wide discrepancy in how individual teachers were implementing the current PA program. The first section of the book also indicates there may be some things we could add to our program to strengthen it. Finally, Paula said she has a friend that teaches Kindergarten in another district who says they have a very strong program and they would be glad to have us come and observe. It was decided to send two people to observe the other district's program. We will meet after the visit has taken place. We will all finish the book and think about what parts apply to us.

11/6/15

The 10/25 meeting had to be cancelled because we couldn't arrange the visit when we would have liked. Paula and Mary reported on the visit to observe the other district program. They described a program that seemed to have several aspects that would benefit our students. One of those aspects was the fact that students who were struggling to acquire PA skills received more instruction that those that were moving along quickly. This kind of obvious change will be difficult due to scheduling issues. Principal O'Brien said she would work on the scheduling problem to see if this would be feasible in our school. Several good ideas were also noted in the book that we would like to incorporate in our new design. We decided that we would need a large block of time to put together all of the new information we had acquired. Principal O'Brien will ask the district for funding for a day of substitutes so we can all work to put this information into a new, more powerful PA program.

11/13/15

Principal O'Brien reports that our request for substitute funding has been approved by the district. We will schedule this day for 12/21/16. In preparation we will do the following:

Paula and Mary will write up the positive aspects of the other district program.

Meghan and Bill will write up the best ideas from the book we all read.

Susan will write up the implementation issues with our present program based on the journals we kept. Everyone with share all of this information with everyone else prior to the 21st.

12/21/15

We worked all day and produced a new, improved (hopefully) PA Awareness Program that we will begin to implement right after the holiday break. Prior to implementing the new program in our classrooms however we will each present a class to the team (10 minutes each) to see if we have a clear, common understanding of what we are striving for. We will do this twice at data team meetings in January.

1/5/16

Each person presented to the group. This was really awkward at first but it was surprising how quickly we got used to watching each other. Comments were really helpful and we all felt we would do much better next time.

1/20/16

Each person presented again. It went so much better! We all improved so much in comfort and actual implementation. As a result of this activity we tweaked the lessons a little bit. The final criteria are listed below:

Standards for Exemplary Implementation of Phonemic Awareness Program in Kindergarten*	
Standard	Criteria to Meet Exemplary Status
Time	-Program is delivered to all students for a minimum of 15 minutes per day. -Students identified as "less ready" receive PA instruction for an additional 10 minutes per day.
Instructional Process	-Instruction in each component begins with the teacher modeling orally accompanied by exaggerated visual stimulus of items engaging to kindergarten children and exaggerated motoric action. -Instructional sequence consists of teacher model; group response repeated at least 3 times; followed by students pairing and sharing at least 3 times using stimulus sets provided by teacher. -During each daily lesson each student is given the opportunity to practice the skill being addressed orally at least 3 times one on one with the teacher. The teacher addresses any necessary correction immediately until student production is correct.

*To be considered exemplary all components must meet identified standard.

We agreed that everyone would begin implementing the new program immediately.

2/6/16

Everyone reports that the new program seems to be going pretty well. We will all take a video of our instruction and score it using the criteria during the next week. All data will be given to Megan in time for our next meeting.

2/15/16

Results of our scoring of video lesson;

Teacher	Five Components Present Meeting Standard				
	1	2	3	4	5
Paula	Yes	No	Yes	No	No
Meghan	Yes	No	No	Yes	No
Bill	Yes	No	No	No	No
Mary	No	Yes	Yes	Yes	Yes
Sally	Yes	No	No	Yes	No

Several issues appear. It looks like component 1 is in pretty good shape. Virtually everyone is struggling with numbers 2 and 5. Mary is an outstanding implementer. Mary has volunteered to video a couple more lessons and make them available for others to study.

3/2/16

Everyone has been working on implementation of the new program. Bill reports that he observed Mary's class twice and finally he gets it. People are finding it difficult to fit in component 5 in the time allocated. We are going to try adding a few minutes to the schedule. The students appear to be responding well to the program, particularly those with more needs. The extra time has been great. We will take some student data prior to the next meeting.

3/20/16

Student data taken last week:

Class	Percent of students meeting standard
Paula	65%
Meghan	57%
Bill	60%
Mary	73%
Sally	55%
	Overall Average 64%

Everyone felt that these numbers were very good for this time of year. Everyone will continue with the program and we will take another snapshot of practice in two weeks just before our next meeting.

Reflection/Response to

Dynamic Improvement Planning

The Dynamic Planning process described in the previous pages is substantially different from the traditional planning process in many ways. What do you see as the positives and negatives of changing to such a process in your district/school? Could you make such a process work for your situation?

_____

_____

_____

_____

_____

_____

_____

_____

_____

_____

_____

_____

_____

_____

_____

_____

_____

_____

_____

_____

_____

_____

Assessment

Assessing the Implementation of Collaborative Teams

When implementing any initiative best practice is to decide how the practice is going to be assessed prior to implementation. By doing so the implementers will not be tempted to structure the assessment process to insure an outcome aligned with their beliefs. The assessment process should remain as objective as possible. For this reason, the team responsible for implementation of collaborative work teams for educators should give serious thought to how the initiative is going to be assessed prior to beginning the implementation. One way to think of this process is to be able to finish the following sentence, "This process will be a success if….."

Fortunately a great deal of information is available to implementers in this regard. In spite of this wealth of assessment devices and information this author would caution against wholesale adoption of any particular scheme. This work is always highly contextual. For this reason it is highly unlikely that any assessment scheme is going to meet your needs perfectly. Therefore it is this author's recommendation that the implementation team review the material available and spend some time crafting a unique assessment scheme suited to your situation.

A final note: A simple, easily understood system is frequently more useful for implementers than a highly complex system. Although you will sacrifice detail, fidelity of implementation and frequency are more important. If a complex system is going to be too difficult to implement, go with a simple assessment and do it faithfully.

In the following pages two contrasting assessment devices are presented. One is a simple, one page rubric and the other is a complex, multi-faceted approach. Both have been used effectively in different situations. Finally a comprehensive document on the topic is referenced that will serve as a useful resource to identify tools to assess your teams.

A Simple Assessment Instrument

Collaborative Team Rubric

	Beginning	Developing	Proficient
Structure	Less than 50% of the meetings are actually held. No agenda, leading to unfocused conversations. Attendance is sporadic. No clear record of tasks is kept.	Meetings are sometimes cancelled or repurposed. Team often has difficulty completing task in time allocated. Often one or more members miss all or part of the meeting. Frequently lose focus during meeting.	Team meetings scheduled well in advance. Meeting length is sufficient Meetings well structured with agenda, minutes, roles. Everyone comes to meeting prepared. Attendance is excellence.
Interactions	Dialogue is frequently unfocused. Instructional practice is rarely discussed. Tensions exist within the group with no resolution. Some members rarely participate.	Dialogue is usually focused primarily on student performance with some discussion of practice. Some members tend to dominate discussion. Disagreements are avoided for the most part but some lie unresolved.	Dialogue is focused on instructional practice and its effect on student performance. All members participate equally. Interpersonal issues are addressed openly, honestly and professionally.
Use of Data	There is no collection of data regarding implementation of strategies or practice. Data concerning student performance is sparse and of questionable validity. There is no discussion of quality of instruction.	Team regularly collects and analyzes data about student performance but rarely collects data about instructional practice. Team relies almost exclusively on anecdotal information concerning instructional practice. Team members are frequently reluctant to comment on practice implementation issues.	Team regularly collects and analyzes objective data about instructional practices and student performance. Student performance data is always related to instructional practice. All data (practice and student) is shared publicly and are basis of team dialogue.

| Actions | Team rarely or never makes decisions concerning instructional practice.

Most decisions team makes concern what students will do, not adults.

Many team decisions appear to have little relationship to improving student performance or instructional practice. | Team sometimes makes decisions concerning instructional practice but rarely articulates performance standards.

Most decisions are based upon team dialogue.

At times it is unclear exactly how the team decision will be implemented.

Decisions are usually related to improving student performance. | Team regularly makes decisions concerning qualities of exemplary instructional practices they will implement and how implementation will be measured.

All decisions are based upon team dialogue.

All decisions are clearly articulated.

All decisions are related to improving student performance. |
|---|---|---|---|

A Comprehensive Assessment Instrument

Assessing the Performance of Instructional Data Teams

(A 360-degree process for a data team to reflect on its performance)

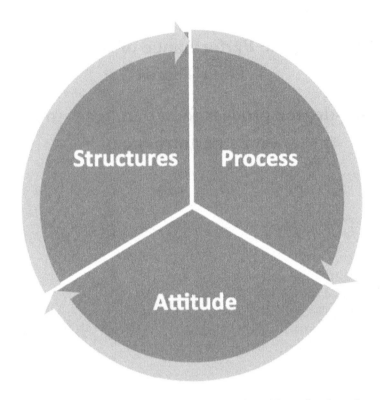

A high functioning data team is a complex entity. To maintain a data team at an optimal level of performance requires constant attention to how the team is functioning. The following documents are designed to provide a structured process by which a data team can periodically assess its functioning level.

The structural characteristics, process standards and holistic view described here are based on working with hundreds of data teams at all levels in all types of schools and districts over 15 years and reflect the author's observation of characteristics and standards of performance associated with the most successful of these teams.

A high functioning data team must demonstrate optimal performance along many dimensions including structural and process dimensions. Deficiencies in either realm can severely inhibit the effectiveness of the team. In addition a new attitude toward the work is required to make the team function at an optimal level. This aspect is captured in the holistic description of an exemplary team.

The enclosed documents can be utilized to assess the performance of both School and Instructional Data Teams.

It is suggested that the team in question begin by reviewing the structural characteristics, process standards and holistic qualities together as a team. The purpose of this review is twofold, first to ascertain that each member of the team has a clear, shared understanding of what each item means and secondly, to allow the team to determine if there is a characteristic, standard or description they feel does not apply to them at this time or if an additional characteristic or standard should be added.

Following this collaborative session, each member of the team should individually complete each document. When all of the individual documents are complete, a member of the team should compile the results. A team meeting should then be held at which the compilation of the individual results are shared and discussed. The team should strive to come to consensus regarding the team's strengths and weaknesses.

Finally a plan to improve should be developed and put into action.

Note: In several "test runs" it has been found that this process does not take much time. Individual team members often complete the process in less than 10 minutes. This seems to be a justified expenditure of time to ensure a high functioning team.

Structural Characteristics of An Effective Data Team

School:_____Team:_____

Date:_____

1. Develops a limited set of enforceable norms. The team posts, reviews and enforces the norms.	
2. Creates a schedule of meetings and sticks to the schedule.	
3. Meets as frequently as possible. At least twice per month. (There is evidence that the frequency of team meetings is directly related to effectiveness)	
4. Identifies three critical roles – facilitator, note taker, timekeeper.	
5. Practices collaboration skills and uses protocols if necessary.	
6. Creates agendas in advance of the meeting and sticks to the agenda.	
7. Bases most of their decisions on facts, research, and data.	
8. Instructional Data Team (IDT) representatives maintain clear communication between School Data Team (SDT) and IDT.	
9. Stays focused in their meetings.	
10. Keeps brief summative minutes of the meeting and distributes them to all 11. members in a timely manner.	
12. Consists of members who come to each meeting fully prepared.	

13. Focuses the majority of their attention on the teacher practice issues not student issues.	
14. Works with their plan in an electronic format and makes the plan available to all staff in the school on an internal network.	
15. Members include: School Team- representatives from all grade levels/departments. Instructional Team – all teachers in Dep't. or grade.	

Place the appropriate symbol next to each statement that you believe best describes the performance of your team.

+ We demonstrate this characteristic on a consistent basis.

0 We demonstrate this characteristic occasionally.

- We never or rarely demonstrate this characteristic.

Process Standards for Data Teams

School:_____Team:_____
Date:_____

1. **The team has identified significant student performance issue(s).**
   - o **Exemplary:**
     The identified issue could be considered to be foundational. If this is not corrected, it will place students' progress at risk.

     The issue affects a significant number of students and it has been longstanding.

   - o **Meeting the Standard:**
     The identified issue is significant, meaning it affects a number of students, it involves an important skill, and it keeps coming up year after year.

   - o **Not Yet Meeting the Standard:**
     The identified issue affects a very small number of students. The issue does not have much leverage. In other words, even if this issue were resolved, it would not have much overall impact on student performance.

   Comments:

   _____
   _____
   _____
   _____
   _____
   _____

2. **The team has gathered data to confirm the issue identified in Step 1.**
    o <u>Exemplary:</u>
       The team has collected data from multiple sources that all point to the issue in a congruent manner. The data is compelling and leaves little room for doubt or error.

    o <u>**Meeting the Standard:**</u>
       The team has collected data that supports the student performance issue identified however the data is limited (1 or 2 sources) and presents some ambiguity.

    o <u>**Not Yet Meeting the Standard:**</u>
       The team has no "hard" data supporting their formulation of the student performance issue. Although there is some reference to data, the data sited is old, and the relationship to the issue is tenuous, requiring assumptions that are not supported.

    Comments:

    _____
    _____
    _____
    _____
    _____

3. **The team has expressed the outcome they hope to have students attain as a SMART goal.**
    o <u>Exemplary:</u>
       Beyond meeting all of the requirements to constitute a SMART goal the team's expression of desired student performance is expressed in a particularly succinct, clear, unambiguous fashion. The goal is undoubtedly highly relevant and compelling. The goal establishes rigorous standards of performance for students.

- **Meeting the Standard:**
  The team has expressed the desired outcome for students in a manner that meets all the criteria demanded by a SMART goal.

- **Not Yet Meeting the Standard:**
  One or more aspects of a SMART goal are not present.

  Comments:

  _____

  _____

  _____

  _____

  _____

  _____

4. **The team identifies interim data to be used to track student progress.**

   - **Exemplary:**
     The team determines the nature of a common formative assessment that will be used to track student progress. This assessment is brief, reliable and clearly related to the goal. The schedule for administration is laid out and is frequent enough to allow the team to adjust their instruction accordingly.

   - **Meeting the Standard:**
     The assessment is common. It is brief and may be reliable. Frequency could be increased. Scheduling is sometimes a problem.

   - **Not Yet Meeting the Standard:**
     Variations appear in administration among teachers. It is to infrequent to inform practice. Scoring is inconsistent.

5.a. The team conducts an analysis of professional practice issues related to achievement of the student SMART goal, identifies a promising practice and presents a rationale for its conclusions.

- o <u>Exemplary:</u>
  The team has conducted a thorough analysis of professional practice issues related to the student SMART goal. There is evidence that the team has considered more than one course of action and evidence that the chosen course offers a likely positive effect on the student issue as demonstrated through the team's research.

- o <u>Meeting the Standard:</u>
  There is evidence in its rationale that the team has considered several aspects of professional practice related to attaining the student goal. There is evidence in the rationale that the area of focus chosen has a documented effect on the desired student outcome.

- o <u>Not Yet Meeting the Standard:</u>
  The rationale does not present evidence that the area of focus chosen has an impact on the desired student outcome.

  Comments:

  _____

  _____

  _____

  _____

  _____

  _____

5.b. The team identifies essential elements of exemplary practice and creates tools to measure implementation.

- o <u>Exemplary:</u>
  The team has identified a limited number of essential elements that constitute exemplary implementation of the practice/strategy. The team has a strategy to measure

implementation in the classroom of each team member.
The team has taken a baseline measure of implementation.

- o **Meeting the Standard:**
  The elements of exemplary implementation contain some
  ambiguity. The team has not taken baseline measure of
  implementation

- o **Not Yet Meeting the Standard:**
  The team has simply stated the strategy or practice with no
  criteria for exemplary implementation.

  Comments:

  _____

  _____

  _____

  _____

  _____

6. The team writes a professional practice SMART goal.

- o **Exemplary:**
  Beyond meeting all of the requirements of a SMART goal
  the team has identified clearly the current level of
  implementation of the practice by team members as well as
  the desired level of practice in such a clear manner as to
  leave no doubt what the team's vision of exemplary
  practice looks like.

- o **Meeting the Standard:**
  The team has expressed the desired change in professional
  practice in a manner that meets all of the criteria
  demanded by a SMART goal.

- o **Not Yet Meeting the Standard:**
  One or more aspects of a SMART goal are missing.

Comments:

_____

_____

_____

_____

_____

7. **The team creates an action plan to meet the identified professional practice goal.**

    o **Exemplary:**

    The action plan clearly describes the major steps the team is taking to achieve the professional practice SMART goal. The actions are unambiguous. Each action has a person responsible for its completion. Each action has a specific time frame for completion. The action steps only go as far as the team can reasonably anticipate.

    o **Meeting the Standard:**

    The action plan contains the major steps needed to meet the goal. The action plan indicates persons responsible and completion dates.

    o **Not Yet Meeting the Standard:**

    It is unclear from the action plan the sequence of events being planned. There is no specific individual identified as responsible for each major step or there are no timelines.

    Comments:

    _____

    _____

    _____

    _____

    _____

8. **The Team implements the plan.**
   o **Exemplary:**
   The team meets all of the criteria in "Meeting the Standard" and in addition the team bases all of its actions on research based information. The team is tracking data concerning implementation by the members as well as outcome data of student progress. The team can articulate the data support for each action they take. The team demonstrates superior collaborative skills, building on each other's ideas. The team meets beyond the scheduled time periods. Team members hold each other accountable for implementing the plan with fidelity.

   o **Meeting the Standard:**
   The team meets on a regular basis to implement the plan. Meetings are scheduled in advance. Agendas are created for each meeting. Minutes are kept of each meeting and sent to members in a timely manner. Every member of the team consistently comes to each meeting prepared. The team collects data on progress toward the professional practice goal as well as the student outcome goal on a regular basis. The team modifies the plan in response to the data. The team files regular progress reports with the School Data Team/District Data Team.

   o **Not Yet Meeting the Standard:**
   If the team fails to meet any of the criteria contained in Meeting the Standard, they are not yet meeting the standard.

   Comments:

   _____

   _____

   _____

   _____

   _____

9. **"Lobbying Up"**
   o <u>**Exemplary:**</u>
   > The team has presented a compelling case, well documented with data and research, to those empowered to make the decision regarding a structural, resource or policy change necessary to accomplish an important student outcome. The team has indicated that they will be persistent and professional in pursuing the implementation of the identified change.

   o <u>**Meeting the Standard:**</u>
   > The team has discussed changes that they feel will need to be made in areas beyond their control and has collected some information to support their position but has yet to formulate any concrete action.

   o <u>**Not Yet Meeting the Standard:**</u>
   > The team has not identified any changes in structure, resources or policy that may be necessary to accomplish an important student outcome.

   > Comments:

   _____

   _____

   _____

   _____

   _____

   _____

Holistic Description of an Exemplary Performing Data Team

An exemplary data team is a group of professional educators who share a strong commitment to the idea that in order to make the changes to their professional practices and school structures that will be necessary to take all students to high levels of achievement, these professional practices and school structural changes need to be identified by the teachers serving the students. These educators recognize that this work will require that they move dramatically to a model of shared rather than isolated practice and that they will have to collaborate in this effort. They understand that this move to collaborative practice means that they will give up a degree of the autonomy they previously enjoyed to the decision-making of the group. These educators also recognize that the actions they take must be based upon the best available information and that their implementation must include data documenting the changes in practice and structure as well as the effects of those changes on student performance. These educators use student data only to identify those aspects of student performance that need to be improved and move quickly to focus their work on changes they (the educators) need to make in order to elicit improved performance by the students. These educators realize that this is a significant change in their roles and responsibilities and are prepared to do whatever it takes to make this work. Finally, these educators demonstrate a strong commitment to the group for accountability for their actions.

What aspects of this description resonate with what our team is already doing?

_____

_____

_____

_____

_____

_____

_____

What aspects of this description are beyond where our team is at this time?

_____
_____
_____
_____
_____
_____
_____
_____

Resource for Assessment Information

"Measurement Instruments for Assessing the Performance of Professional Learning Communities." Blitz, Cynthia, L., Schulman, Rebecca, Rutgers University. Institute of Educational Sciences, U.S. Department of Education. Mid-Atlantic Regional Educational Laboratory, September 2016,

Reflection/Response to Assessment

As you think about how you wish to assess the effectiveness of your collaborative teams, what aspects of their implementation do you feel are of the highest priority at this time and in the near term? What approach do you think would work best in your situation to give you the most helpful information regarding the operation of your teams?

_____

_____

_____

_____

_____

_____

_____

_____

_____

_____

_____

_____

_____

_____

_____

_____

_____

_____

_____

_____

_____

_____

_____

Impediments to Successful Implementation

Impediments to Successful Implementation

Creating and maintaining high quality collaborative teams in a school or district is a formidable challenge. This author has worked in dozens of schools and districts that have undertaken this work. All but a handful have been unable to take full advantage of the benefits that can be derived from the process. In the section that follows, a number of observed impediments to successful implementation are discussed. Being aware of these obstacles may prepare the reader to plan for these challenges.

Obvious Impediments

Lack of active administrative support/trust:

Sustained implementation of a process as significant as large-scale collaboration among educators has little chance of success in the absence of knowledgeable, active support of leadership at all levels of the organization. This consultant has never seen a system achieve meaningful implementation of this process where the senior leadership displays either disinterest or outright hostility. Staff is quick to note if the leadership is encouraging them to change to a more collaborative interaction style while they themselves maintain a rigid, top down authoritarian style. This situation is fairly obvious in its negative impact on sustained, meaningful implementation. This is not to say however that at least initially, until a critical mass of staff come to understand the benefits of moving to a more collaborative practice that some directive actions won't be necessary by leadership to "get the ball moving". However, if this rigid, top down style persists the result will be negative.

More subtle and somewhat less obvious is a situation in which leadership at the district and/or school level displays indifference. This is also more common. The attitude seems to be that this would be good for teachers to do but only if it means the leader won't have to do anything different. Both approaches practically guarantee at best, shallow, superficial implementation and therefore minimal student impact.

The active leadership required involves the leaders becoming as or more knowledgeable about the collaborative process and benefits as the staff. It means the leaders attending the training sessions (the entire session) and assisting to solve the inevitable implementation issues that will arise. Many of the implementation issues such as creating more meaningful and protected time for collaboration to take place are beyond the reach of staff and will require senior leadership to make significant efforts to accomplish. Absent a deep understanding of the value of collaboration and the potential for improved student performance few leaders will extend the needed effort.

Reflection: In thinking about your situation, do you feel that you have the level of commitment from leadership at both the district and school level to implement and sustain a quality collaborative process in your school/district?   If not, what steps can you take to change this situation?

Insufficient Time:

The single greatest barrier to implementing a significant collaborative structure and sustaining it is the lack of time for educators to meet together to do this work.   Research by Linda Darling Hammond has found that many developed countries around the world allocate over 50% of a teachers contractual time to non-classroom work, including collaborative improvement of practice.   In the United States teachers average over 80% of their contractual time in their own classrooms. This simple fact almost guarantees an isolated work force. (Darling-Hammond, et al., 2009).   This issue is so critical that this consultant advises districts and schools that if they cannot devote at least 1 hour every other week to collaborative work to get started, then they should consider not beginning the process.   The fact of the matter is that this work takes a great deal of time if it is to be done correctly.   Giving teachers training in the process and getting hopes up about the outcomes possible only to have the process sabotaged by a lack of meaningful time will only contribute to teachers' well founded cynicism about "just another meaningless initiative".   Many districts observed by this consultant are not doing professional learning communities or data teams, they are doing "fake" communities and teams and the number one reason they are "fake" is that there is not a realistic amount of time available.

Professional Learning in The Learning Profession: A Status Report on Teacher Development in the United States and Abroad. Linda Darling-Hammond, Ruth Chung Wei, Alethea Andree, Nikole Richardson & Stelios Orphanos. School Redesign Network at Stanford University, National Staff Development Council, 2009.

Reflection: Do you have enough time in your schedule for your educators to enter into meaningful collaboration? If not, how will you create the time needed?

_____

_____

_____

_____

_____

_____

Toxic Environment:

Fortunately this situation is relatively rare. Some district/school environments are so toxic that no initiative, including implementation of collaboration has much of a chance of success. From political toxicity to aggressive, negative management/staff issues to such severe financial issues that basic services are not available all make situations into which an initiative as large and comprehensive as moving to a collaborative structure doomed before it starts. It is always amazing to this consultant that in situations like these this initiative is even attempted.

Reflection: Is your district/school in a position to implement a more collaborative structure and have a chance of success? Are relationships and finances stable enough to sustain the challenges that will be presented as implementation proceeds? If there is such a major impediment to successful implementation what needs to happen first before implementation is even attempted?

_____

_____

_____

_____

_____

_____

Lack of Support of Policymakers:

As cited in the next section, a change from a structure dominated by "private practice" by teachers to a more collaborative practice is a significant cultural change for most schools and/or districts. Since most schools or districts are overseen by a Board of Education or other political leaders who have all experienced schooling in the dominant cultural context, they must be brought to a level of understanding of the benefits of such change. If this issue is not addressed in a thoughtful and respectful manner with policymakers, they can undo any such initiative in short order. Anyone advocating such a change should ask themselves, "If people who are upset about this change should approach the policymakers, are these policymakers prepared to support the initiative?" Unfortunately, it is not uncommon for policymakers to learn about an initiative to move to a more collaborative structure only after the initiative is underway and those aggrieved by the change make their views known. A far better strategy is to inform and educate these policymakers from the outset so they are prepared to respond to possible concerns in an informed and articulate manner. Some will argue that such education of policymakers is too time consuming and many of them will be disinterested. And in fact it may never become an issue. However, if it does become an issue and as an advocate you are placed in a defensive stance, the time and effort will be compounded.

Another issue concerns a significant change in policymakers such as in an election that sees a new chief executive or new board elected. Although many times this will not affect such an initiative, this writer has witnessed entire programs wiped out in such situations. At such times it is be helpful if there have been public pronouncements of support based upon strong evidence and that the initiative has been widely supported by parents and teachers.

Reflection: Are the policymakers in your school/district knowledgeable and supportive of your efforts to increase the level of collaboration among your staff? If a challenge to the initiative was presented to your policymakers how do you think they would respond? What actions could you take to shore up policymaker support?

_____

_____

_____

_____

_____

_____

_____

_____

_____

_____

_____

_____

_____

_____

_____

_____

Not So Obvious Impediments

In the collaborative data team process described by this author, step 5 requires the team to examine some aspect of their current practice that is contributing to the less than desirable student performance identified by the team. This step has proven to be a formidable hurtle for many teams. The purpose of this section is to examine some more subtle reasons for this difficulty and to offer some suggestions for the team to consider in order to resolve the issues.

Lack of Awareness:

A surprising number of teachers and school administrators are simply unaware of the evidence concerning the powerful, positive effects on student achievement with increased collaboration. Observation has revealed a few common reasons for this lack of awareness.

Many educators today are completely overwhelmed by the day-to-day management of their school and classrooms. Particularly in schools with more challenging student populations, the myriad of social, behavioral, and academic problems that large numbers of students bring into school each day requires such constant and intense effort that little time or energy remains to study and reflect on any strategy or structure regardless of how successful it may prove. Many of these schools, particularly those with dwindling resources, resemble more closely a hospital emergency room than a serious place of learning with a constant flow of issues that continually interrupt all activities. Under these circumstances staff is frequently exhibiting heroic efforts just to maintain a sense of order and safety.

In less challenging schools teachers and administrators are frequently confronted with a large number of initiatives, (not of their choosing) all of which are to be implemented simultaneously and all of which promise dramatic positive results. With inadequate time and resources, the staff does what it can in a compliant manner knowing full well that the implementation will be shallow and largely ineffective. This process is often repeated in a cyclical manner. As a result, school personnel can become somewhat cynical concerning any initiative that is supposed to "improve student outcomes" and virtually tune out any initiative. This "tuning out", while understandable under the conditions, has led to a common situation where staffs become uninformed about truly significant strategies that could improve their effectiveness. Under these circumstances teachers have been observed to retreat to a focus on their own classrooms and the construction of their own lessons.

Collaboration and its positive effects on student performance has been observed to be one of the victims of this "tuning out" behavior.

It is therefore the responsibility of anyone hoping to move a school community to a more collaborative culture to proceed with caution and respect for the opinions of the staff. One way to conceptualize this process is that the leader of the initiative needs to convince the staff with concrete evidence that this is an initiative worth pursuing.

Use the space below to capture your thoughts about the above. Does this resonate with your experience? How would you proceed to make the implementation of collaborative work more successful than other initiatives?

_____

_____

_____

_____

_____

_____

_____

_____

_____

_____

_____

_____

_____

_____

_____

_____

_____

Historical And Structural Traditions:

We begin this examination with a brief review of the historical and cultural development of public schooling that has brought us to this point. This is important due to the fact that these historical and cultural "norms" for how schools function are powerful levers in defining the roles of various players in the system. These unofficial "norms" have evolved over generations and are widely understood. After all, virtually everyone has experienced the system and to some degree at least has experienced it under these cultural "norms".

One of the most powerful of these unofficial "norms" as to how schools operate is the notion that students are the primary variable in the acquisition or lack of acquisition of knowledge and skills. If a student or group of students struggle to acquire a set of skills the assumption frequently has been that the student didn't try hard enough or the student wasn't interested enough or the student didn't display the discipline or behavior necessary to stick with it or that the student simply did not have the intellectual ability or was in some way disabled.

This type of thinking, which was widely accepted as fact by all segments of the educational community and culture contributed to the widespread and extremely homogeneous structure of schools where knowledge and skills to be acquired by students are strictly articulated and apportioned over a very rigid grade structure. A specific set of acquisition expectations are set for each grade and content area and a fixed time line is developed within which these skills are to be acquired by all students of a certain age. The theory goes that if all parties to the endeavor uphold their part of the bargain then the vast majority of students will succeed; policymakers and administrators will build the structure and provide resources, teachers will present the material to the students, students will attend, behave appropriately, follow directions and put in as much effort as is required and parents will support the efforts of the school both directly and indirectly but most importantly by ensuring that their children do everything they are supposed to do as students.

Although this system never did work successfully for all students, that was not the point. One of the primary goals of the system was to sort students into groups – primarily those capable of high quality advanced academic work and those less capable. And as long as there was a viable option for those students who were less capable – namely high wage/low skilled work – there was no incentive on anyone's part to change the bargain. The system was working as it was designed to work.

One of the major advantages of this system was that it was relatively inexpensive. The structure was static, the skills required of teachers were relatively low and this helped to keep wages low. Additionally, keeping the students engaged and motivated fell more on the parents and students than the system. The system worked "effectively" and efficiently for a very long time. As a matter of fact, this system continues to work effectively in many places today.

With the dramatic and rapid reduction of the low skill/high wage alternative for students unsuccessful in this system stress on the system began to increase. (This stress culminated in the somewhat strange mandate by the federal government that 100% of students must be successful in the system by 2014-No Child Left Behind).

As people began casting about for solutions to the problem of getting more students to be successful in the current system they largely avoided looking at the larger systemic, structural issues and instead focused on the two primary players – teachers and students.

With regard to the teachers, the idea was that teachers required more education, which would make them more effective. Therefore over the last 100 plus years the qualifications to become a teacher went from possessing a high school diploma to possessing a master's degree.

With regard to the students this led to a decade's long search into answering the question, "What is wrong with these students that causes them to be unable to succeed in this system?" One of the major consequences of this line of inquiry has been the explosive growth of special education. In effect the answer to the question posed above turned out to be, "Yes, there is something wrong with these students. They are disabled." And as such, they required a level of instruction that was beyond the capability of most "regular" educators, even with their advanced degrees.

While both of these strategies saw some tangible benefits, given the amount of money and resources that have been allocated over the years one could easily conclude that the results have been meager.

The problem is that in spite of these two strategies, the basic structure was never addressed. Policymakers and administrators still build (or maintain) the structure and provide (more or less) the resources, teachers are expected to present the material, students are still expected to attend and behave and parents are still expected to ensure that their children do what they need to do.

So now what happens when students do not behave as they need to in order to be successful and/or parents don't or can't ensure that their children do what they need to do?

In the past couple of decades public policy has evolved to the point that the systems can no longer simply refuse to accept responsibility for these non-conforming students and their ineffective or helpless parents. While policymakers have been somewhat strident in this position, they have been equally strident concerning what they will not change. They have shown little or no interest in attacking the underlying problems with these students and their families, which are usually conditions related to poverty. They have been equally disinterested in changing the long standing traditional rigid structure of the educational system including such things as calendars, daily schedules, the graded structure, isolated teachers, age groupings, time as the constant and achievement as the variable, etc. The one variable that policymakers have been willing to look at, at least in a superficial manner has been teachers. The view has been incredibly simplistic – "failing" students must be caused by "failing" teachers. Thus, the strategy has been to identify the "failing" teachers and replace them with "successful", "effective" (put whatever descriptor here you choose) teachers and you will produce more "successful" students. Of course this is done in a complete vacuum with no consideration for possibly changing the structures within which these teachers work or the circumstances in which the students live.

It should be no wonder then that teachers might be somewhat defensive when someone says to them, "If the students are not succeeding you (the teachers) have to accept responsibility and change your tactics, approaches, and/or practices, but don't ask us to change anything else."

Given all of the above, that defensiveness and unwillingness is certainly understandable. However, the stance of not being willing to change anything is not acceptable either. As not only the adults in the situation, but as the professional educators in the situation, teachers must be willing to change and learn on a continuous basis in order to maximize the success of as many students as possible. This being said, teachers must also be willing to articulate and stand up for changes to those structural and historical conditions that limit the degree to which they can make the changes they need to make in order for their lessons to be more effective for more students.

One of these changes that teachers need to demand is more time to collaborate and learn with their colleagues about how to be more successful with more students. The evidence concerning the benefits of collaborative problem solving for teachers is overwhelming. Why is it then that teachers, who are being pressured to be more successful with more students, are not pressing for more time dedicated to such collaboration? Why are they not demanding an end to being forced to acquire and pay for advanced degrees in order to keep their jobs when the evidence of the efficacy of this practice is overwhelming in its lack of effect on more teachers being more successful with more students?

One way to begin to effect a change in this fundamental structure of schools is for teachers, working in collaborative teams, to take on the challenge of finding ways to become more successful with more students by working together to find more and more effective approaches and strategies. Given the very limited time and structure available for this work at this time, changes and gains will be modest. But success leads to more success. Armed with numerous examples of success with the process, teachers can lobby (demand) for more dramatic structural changes to increase their effectiveness.

Use the space below to capture your thoughts concerning the above.

_____

_____

_____

_____

_____

It's Working For Some Students:

Teachers look at a group of students who are not responding positively to the instruction they are receiving. At the same time however these same teachers in these same classrooms see a group of students who are responding very positively to the same instruction. At the same time these teachers frequently see behavioral and attitudinal differences between these two groups with the successful group demonstrating far more "successful" student behaviors (engaged, attentive, compliant, behaved, etc.) than the unsuccessful group. Under such circumstances it is understandable that many teachers would conclude that there is nothing wrong with their instruction, the problem is the students. When someone suggests that it is the teachers' problem; that all students must respond successfully to the instruction they are receiving, if the teachers are willing to entertain the idea at all, it frequently will be through the lens of changing the behavioral characteristics of unsuccessful students so that they demonstrate more "successful" student behavior. This may lead to an in-depth analysis of the learning and behavioral profile of the unsuccessful students and the development of an intervention plan designed to change the students' "unsuccessful student profile" to be more like a "successful student profile". (The very rational thinking here being that if we can instill more "successful" student characteristics in these students then they will respond more positively to the instruction.) In many cases this approach does lead to improved performance on the part of some students. This success reinforces the belief that in fact the problem is the student.

If this approach did solve the problem and make the vast majority of students successful in all teachers' classrooms this discussion would not even be taking place. The fact of the matter is that despite tremendous efforts devoted to this approach, and some true successes, large numbers of students remain unsuccessful in these classrooms. This fact should lead professional educators to give serious attention then to the other major variable in the instruction/learning equation, the instruction. If the evidence suggests that a significant number of students are exhibiting difficulty learning from the current instruction, we have to consider changing the instruction. At the same time we can acknowledge that some of these students may require intensive efforts to change their "unsuccessful" student behaviors. These two approaches need not be mutually exclusive.

Use the space below to capture your thoughts concerning the above.

_____

_____

_____

_____

_____

_____

_____

_____

_____

It Is Not My Job:

In some schools and school systems there is a strong culture that it is simply not the role of the teachers to know how to change their instruction in order to better meet the needs of the students. This responsibility lies with policy-makers, administrators and other levels of management. Teachers, being at the bottom of this hierarchal pyramid are only expected to implement the instruction and programs that are developed or identified by their superiors. All responsibility for the identification of these strategies as well as the training required of the teachers to ensure implementation is their responsibility. If such things do not occur it is the superiors' responsibility. This is an old-fashioned idea that was part of the top down, Tayloristic organization of many school systems. Teachers were viewed as relatively unskilled workers who needed to be supervised closely to adhere to the work rules agreed to by their bargaining agent and management. In this scenario "management", who was solely responsible for their success or failure, made all major decisions concerning what would be taught and how it would be taught. Teachers were simply implementers. Even in systems that have moved beyond this unsuccessful model, there are often remnants of this attitude found among many teachers. In such cases the leaders involved must work to acknowledge the genesis of these attitudes but persistently and respectfully push teachers into a more professional stance. Frequently newer teachers who did not experience such a model are allies in helping to evolve a more enlightened attitude. Leaders must also examine policies and traditions in schools that reinforce these top down attitudes and work to eliminate them since these provide prima face evidence to teachers that things have in fact not changed.

Use the space below to capture your thoughts concerning the above.

_____

_____

_____

_____

_____

_____

_____

_____

_____

_____

_____

_____

It Is Wrong Or Bad Practice To Do This:

This reason is encountered much more frequently at the secondary level.

Many teachers truly feel that it is inappropriate or "bad practice" to change strategies when students do not demonstrate acquisition of the material taught. To these teachers it would be irresponsible on their part to "coddle" students in this manner. These teachers feel that it is a major responsibility to teach students that, "things do not always come easy", or that, "the real world is not going to change just for you." In addition, these teachers believe that students must be taught that there are consequences for their actions. In other words, if students are not going to put in the effort necessary, even if they do not find the activity interesting or engaging and as a result they fail, then they deserve to fail and that is an important lesson.

To these teachers the idea that their instruction may be "boring" or uninteresting to their students is irrelevant. They believe their job is not to "entertain" students. They believe that some things are boring and difficult in life and that students need to just get used to that. These teachers see it as part of their duty to teach students to persevere even in the face of tedious or meaningless (to the student) work.

An effective strategy to address this situation is to acknowledge that there is an element of truth to the above. Students do need to learn that not everything will be easy or exciting. It is a matter of proportion. If the leader acknowledges this as a strategy the teacher is employing to achieve a goal (students learn that everything isn't easy and thus engage when it is not exciting) then the proof is in the effectiveness of the strategy in achieving the goal. If teachers can show that by failing students for their behavior it results in a change in behavior, then it is an effective strategy. However, if teachers end up repeatedly failing students and the students' behavior does not change, then that is evidence that the strategy did not work. In a system that expects teachers to exhibit high levels of professional behavior, repeatedly implementing the same strategy, in the face of evidence of its ineffectiveness, is not acceptable.

Use the space below to capture your thoughts concerning the above.

_____

_____

_____

_____

_____

_____

_____

_____

_____

_____

I'd Like To Do This But I Just Don't Have The Time:

In many schools and school systems this is absolutely true. Many if not most schools and school systems continuously engage in what Douglas Reeves has labeled, "Initiative Fatigue"*. Systems and schools, with the best of intentions, are attempting to implement far too many initiatives at the same time, while drastically underestimating the learning curve required of the people (usually teachers) to adequately implement each. Rarely does this writer go into a school that has less than four major initiatives on the agenda. There is usually something about a new or improved literacy program and maybe a new math program as well. There is also a new social learning skills program and a new program to challenge English Language Learners or gifted students. Usually each program is valuable and desirable. Teachers and principals are observed making valiant efforts to implement each program. The fact of the matter is that given the amount of time these teachers and principals are given to learn new strategies or programs, they can usually do no more than engage in superficial implementation of these programs and as a result of diffusing their efforts to such an extent may cause more harm than good. How many times have teachers been provided with a day of in-service training concerning a significant change in instruction, handed a book at the end of the day and be expected to implement the program immediately?

Leaders need to directly confront teacher's legitimate concerns about time. If we are going to expect teachers to enter into collaborative problem solving work as described here we are going to have to provide them with a significant period of time to do this work.

This writer has specifically recommended to schools that if they are unable to allocate at least 60 uninterrupted minutes every other week for this work they would be better off pursuing something else that requires less time.

*Reeves, D. (2006). The Learning Leader. Alexandria, VA: Association for Supervision and Curriculum Development.

Use the space below to capture your thoughts concerning the above.

_____
_____
_____
_____
_____
_____
_____
_____
_____

In All Honesty, I Don't Know Another Way To Teach This:

Perhaps this issue should not even be included here. When a group of teachers cease to insist there is nothing wrong with their instruction and that the lack of achievement lies elsewhere, this group is ready to move.

This writer has frequently asked teachers how they would approach teaching a particular concept differently if they discovered that their original attempt was largely unsuccessful. It is not unusual for these teachers to flounder at this point to articulate another meaningful approach beyond repeating their original instruction. This should not be surprising. The expectations for teachers to expand their instructional repertoire are meager in most schools. This low expectation coupled with the fact that teachers are not provided with the time or a structure to carry out such work practically ensures it does not occur.

It is recommended to leaders at this point that they refrain from telling the teachers what they should do. Rather, leaders should suggest that teachers need to find the answer themselves. Several data team meeting times spent in the library, or meeting with an expert searching for alternative approaches is usually very fruitful. It has been this writer's experience that teachers respond very positively to this respectful acknowledgement of their professionalism. It has also been my experience that teachers in almost every case have come up with viable alternatives. We would criticize a teacher who simply gave the students the answer each time they encountered a problem. The same is true here. A bit of "collaborative productive struggle" on the part of the teachers will pay large dividends.

Of course the cry from many is that we don't have the time to indulge in such activities. To those who say this I would respond, "How has your current approach been working for you?" Giving teachers time to find their own answers to their own instructional problems in their particular context will be far more effective than a generalized solution they don't own.

Use the space below to capture your thoughts concerning the above.

_____

_____

_____

_____

_____

_____

_____

_____

_____

_____

_____

_____

_____

_____

_____

_____

_____

_____

I Like To Work Alone:

Teaching is an isolated profession. And it has been for a long time. It should perhaps be no surprise that teaching therefore attracts a number of people who prefer to work alone.

Many teachers feel that they cannot be bound by any particular set of actions while working in their classrooms. They feel that they must be free to adjust all of their instruction "on the fly" or "in the moment" in order to meet the unique needs of the students in front of them at that exact time. This "Teacher as Artist" idea used to be more common but is still prevalent in many schools today. At the post secondary level it is enshrined in the idea of "academic freedom".

It will be unusual for a teacher or group of teachers to openly espouse this idea but it may lie at the heart of a reluctance to enter into a collaborative situation. The following tactic has been found to be helpful when this attitude appears to be prevalent.

The point to be made is that in fact most of a teacher's practice will remain private. After all, in the collaborative practice being described here we are only asking teachers to take a slice of their practice and give up their complete autonomy to the group. The bulk of their practice will still remain under their sole control. This fact alone will assuage many. And when teachers see that their effectiveness is in fact enhanced through collaboration all but the most reluctant will be won over.

This is another situation where if the participation is voluntary it is very helpful. If complete voluntary participation is not possible, then letting teachers choose with whom they will collaborate is better than forcing a team together. Having 2 Algebra I teams of 3 people each may be quite preferable to 1 team of 6.

In practical terms, although some teachers may have been teaching alongside each other for years, a level of animosity may exist between them that makes any collaboration almost impossible. In such rare cases it is probably best not to force the issue.

Use the space below to capture your thoughts concerning the above:

Implementation for Success and Sustainability

Implementation for Success and Sustainability

Two very similar schools embark on the implementation of collaborative work structures for teachers. It doesn't matter if the school calls this work Professional Learning Communities (PLC's) or Data Teams. In both cases the school leadership has read the literature and has been convinced that if teachers enter into a structured, collaborative problem solving process they will improve the effectiveness of their instruction.

Both schools provide similar amounts of professional development to their teachers in order to familiarize them with the specific collaborative process they have selected. Knowing that this type of up-front professional development is insufficient to ensure proper implementation, both schools have also employed expert coaching services to work with their staff to ensure that the ideas contained in the model are actually implemented. The amount and quality of this coaching is similar in each school.

As both schools measure their implementation using rubrics designed for the purpose they both score high on understanding and implementing all of the features contained in the model.

After two years of implementation the data from the two schools regarding changes in student performance tells a very different story. School A has seen the beginnings of a dramatic turnaround in student performance while school B has seen little or no change. The question is: Why this difference in effect on student learning when both schools with very similar student makeup and very similar roll-out of this initiative?

Having seen this scenario a number of times this writer has concluded that there are a number of factors lying beneath the surface that are critical in determining the effectiveness of this initiative. As in the case cited above a school can do all of the right things on the surface, provide the training, provide the follow-up coaching, provide the resources, even score high on implementation measures and still not realize the positive effect of the initiative. In the following paragraphs some of these critical underlying issues will be addressed.

Issue Number 1. Commitment:

If the teachers involved in learning how to work collaboratively are not truly committed to the idea it will have little effect. Teachers simply have too much control over what actually happens day to day in their classrooms for any initiative to which they are not actually committed to have much effect. The question any leader should ask is, "Would they do this if they didn't have to?" or "Would they do this if I did not insist on it?" If the answer to this question remains, "no" after people have learned how to do the process then the process will have little effect. The leader's job is not to force or intimidate teachers to change their practice but to convince them or even better, to inspire them to change their practice to become more collaborative. Experience has shown the surest way to garner this type of commitment from teachers is to have them see the benefits of the process in the performance of their students. This can be accomplished by guiding teams to some quick wins by attacking "low hanging fruit". Initially, rather than attempting to improve the level of implementation of a sophisticated reading process which may take months or years, the team might first be encouraged to find a more effective way to manage practice sessions for learning multiplication facts. Of course this will vary based upon the experience and sophistication of the team members. The point is that paying attention to the teachers' real commitment to the process is important. Teachers are usually polite and compliant. If they are just following the process because it is the administration's latest fad, it will fail.

Response to Issue Number 1: Use the space below to capture your thoughts regarding issue number 1 and strategies you might use to ensure a high level of teacher commitment to increased collaboration.

_____

_____

_____

_____

_____

_____

_____

_____

Issue Number 2: Active Leadership:

Particularly at the beginning of the process before teacher commitment has been solidified, active leadership is vital to the process.

At the district level this means that senior leadership is directly involved in the work. Senior leaders (superintendent, assistant superintendent, directors, etc.) are communicating to the policy makers and ensuring their support through education and demonstration. Without support at the policy maker level the initiative can be swept away at a moments notice. At the same time the district actively demonstrates its support of and involvement in the initiative by becoming the local experts. An outside consultant can be the expert on the subject but the district leadership must become the experts at implementing the initiative in their particular school district. This local expertise demonstrates a commitment to the initiative that speaks louder than any speeches or memos. And by acquiring this level of internal expertise, district leadership ensures sustainability.

At the school level the school principal is an active, regular supporter of the process. The principals who are successful at getting the process implemented in their schools really believe in the process. They are not doing it simply because it is a directive from above (the staff can always tell). These principals are creative and energized about solving the host of logistic problems that arise in most schools when they attempt to create sufficient time for teachers to collaborate. These principals are active participants in the data team process itself particularly the school data team and sometimes at the instructional data team level as well. These principals are able to strike a balance between giving teachers as much authority as they are ready to assume while gradually moving them to greater and greater decision-making levels. Finally, these principals are active in lobbying at the district level for making structural changes necessary to support the process as well as for programs their teams identify that are beyond the control of the school.

Response to Issue Number 2: Use the space below to capture your thoughts regarding issue number 2 and strategies you might use to ensure a high level of active leadership at both the district and school levels.

_____

_____

_____

_____

_____

_____

_____

_____

Issue Number 3: Trust or Psychological Safety:

A multi-year investigation into what characterizes successful collaborative teams by Google (Project Aristotle 2016)* led them to conclude that a major factor in successful teams was that they created an environment that was psychologically safe for the members. This issue has been studied for many years and consistent findings are that although teams may differ in many, many characteristics, successful teams are almost always places where the members can feel safe expressing their opinions, challenging other's opinions and being challenged, all in service to accomplishing the team's goals. I have called this trust. Members of successful teams trust one another to treat them respectfully and fairly. This is particularly important for the relationship between the principal and the teachers. The principal will have to trust the teachers to do the right thing. If the principal has a disrespectful attitude toward a significant number of the teachers the process will fail. If the principal feels that teachers will make decisions in their own self interest and not the interest of the students the process will fail. This is not to say that at times the principal will not disagree with the teachers. This is expected since the principal brings a different perspective to the work. How this disagreement is handled however is critical. If it is done in a respectful, professional and factual manner where all concerned can remain psychologically safe it can actually make the team stronger.

* Duhigg, Charles. (February 28, 2016). Group Study. New York Times Magazine. P.21.

Response to Issue Number 3: Use the space below to capture your thoughts regarding issue number 3 and strategies you might use to ensure a high level of trust or psychological safety in your teams.

Issue Number 4: Time:

When teachers begin to deconstruct an instructional strategy it is going to take time. If the school cannot create a sufficient amount of time for the teachers to do this work the process will fail because teachers will not be able to be successful. Based upon work with hundreds of teams over more than 15 years this writer has come to believe that if the school cannot create at least 60 minutes of uninterrupted work time every other week for a collaborative team the school may be better off postponing implementation of collaborative teams until such time is available. Research by Douglas Reeves has clearly indicated that the more time teachers have for this work the more successful they usually are.

Many schools create this time by hiring substitute teachers to cover classes while they meet. This is frequently the only option available to a school and it does work. However, it is this author's experience that when teams meet while the students are in the school it always distracts their attention and interferes with their ability to thoughtfully approach this work (student issues will always be the priority). A far better solution is to make the time available when students are not present either through extending the teacher contractual day, releasing the students early or some combination of both.

Finally, whatever time is made available must be protected. In most schools there are many competing agendas for teachers' time (faculty meetings, parent issues, student concerns, personal planning time, etc.). I have seen some schools create a schedule of biweekly data team meetings only to co-opt meeting time on a regular basis. Again, if you can't create enough time, don't start until you can. Don't put this process in place just because it is fashionable. If you aren't committed enough to the process to give it the resources it needs (time), do something else.

Response to Issue Number 4: *Use the space below to capture your thoughts regarding issue number 4 and strategies you might use to ensure that the collaborative teams you create will have enough time to be successful.*

_____

_____

_____

_____

_____

_____

_____

_____

_____

_____

_____

Issue Number 5. Structure:

Getting just the right amount of structure for the process to succeed can be a difficult thing. The process must be structured in such a manner that it is efficient and thoughtful but not so much that teams spend the majority of their time filling out forms. Again, based upon years of experience and making virtually every mistake, the following recommendations as to structure are made:

A simple agenda is sent to members in advance. This is basically a heads-up regarding what will be discussed. This is particularly important if people need to bring data or other material to the meeting. In many schools today this is done electronically.

A simple, brief process for recording what happened at the meeting is a necessity. People are busy and will frequently need a reminder. Anything more than a few paragraphs will not be read. Again, in many schools today this is done electronically (See Dynamic Planning).

Roles: Someone will have to take responsibility for facilitating the meeting. Someone will have to be responsible for making sure the critical points are recorded in some way. The same person cannot do both. It is very common to rotate these roles. They do not need to be formal. The principal should not always be the facilitator; as a matter of fact this is usually a bad idea.

Response to Issue Number 5: Use the space below to capture your thoughts regarding issue number 5 and strategies you might use to create just enough structure for your teams to operate efficiently and effectively.

_____

_____

_____

_____

_____

_____

_____

_____

_____

_____

_____

_____

Issue Number 6: Practice:

For many teachers, both veteran and novice this is a new process. It is also a professionally demanding process. It is not easy. For these reasons, teams will need time to improve. It will be unusual for a team to do this very well in the beginning. People may feel uncomfortable in new roles. People may not know exactly what to do. People may need to take time to get used to working with each other and creating the psychologically safe environment. For all of these reasons and more everyone involved needs to understand that the team will evolve. Richard Elmore once said that the only way people get better at this work is to do the work (Elmore, 2004). In the case of collaborative teams this is very true; all of this being said, it is a good practice for the team to periodically engage in a self reflective process to ascertain their progress at getting better. There are a number of very good tools available that teams can use for this purpose (See Assessment Section). The recommendation here is that no tool will fit the team's purpose perfectly. The team should look at various tools for ideas and then create their own.

Elmore, Richard. (2004). School Reform form the Inside Out. Cambridge, MA. Harvard Education Press. Number 7.

Response to Issue Number 6: Use the space below to capture your thoughts regarding issue number 6 and how you might plan for teams to get the practice they need and to ensure that they make continuous progress.

_____

_____

_____

_____

_____

_____

_____

_____

Issue Number 7: Moral Purpose:

This could be called the missing element in many attempts to move systems to more collaborative work. John Kotter would talk about a "sense of urgency"(Kotter, 2008). In education an underlying moral purpose appears to be a more compelling argument. What is meant here is that the leadership needs to create a driving moral purpose for asking people to change their practice. A personal story here to illustrate the point:

This author was involved in moving a system to more collaborative work. Data concerning the less than desired performance of our students was presented and the likely positive effects of a change to more collaborative work was detailed. The data was dramatic and compelling but still the staff did not seem to be energized. Exhortations as to how we needed to make a serious change did not seem to be working. Then at one meeting this author played video interviews he had conducted with 5 incoming kindergarten children. Each child when asked what they were going to learn in school said the same thing with enthusiasm and innocence, "I am going to learn how to read!" The audience of teachers all smiled and chuckled. Then the system's performance data was placed next to the pictures of the children accompanied by the following comment. "As you can all see, our evidence shows that only 3 of these 5 children are actually going to learn to read well." It is up to each of us to change this figure and give all of our children the education they need." You could hear a pin drop in the room. From that moment on the attitude changed.

Teachers respond well to the moral purpose involved in teaching children. It is more than a job. This issue helps to understand the frequent situation where a group of educators are apparently doing all of the right things regarding collaboration but it just feels hollow. If a unifying moral or ethical purpose is not associated with the change in practice it can become just a set of routine practices that are repeated according to a script.

The implementation team should consider seriously how to connect the change to more collaborative practice to a meaningful moral or ethical purpose relevant to their unique situation.

Kotter, John P. (2008.). A sense of Urgency. Cambridge MA. Harvard University Press.

Response to issue number 7: Use the space below to capture your thoughts regarding issue number 7 and how you might go about infusing a moral purpose to and for the implementation of collaborative work:

_____

_____

_____

_____

_____

_____

_____

Structures for Collaborative Teams

In a School

Structure for a Small School

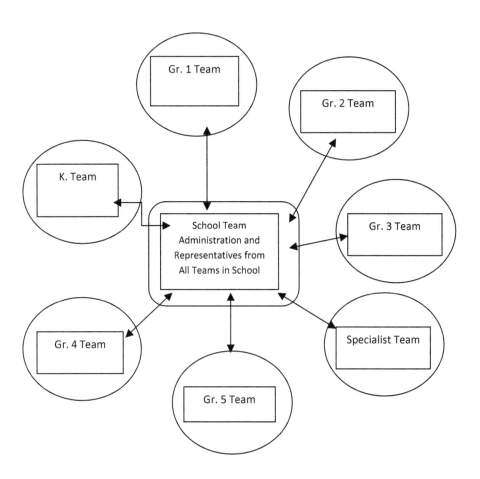

Structure for a Large School

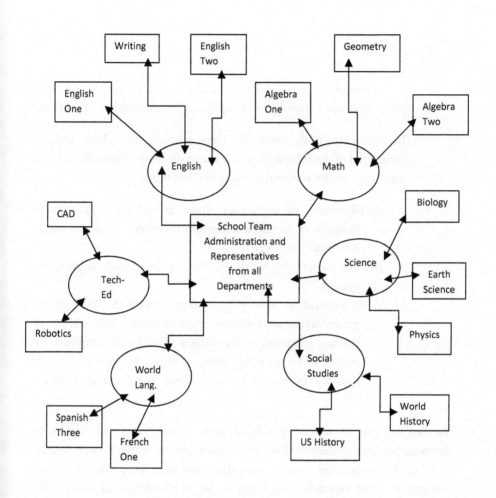

The structures for collaborative teams presented on the previous pages have been found to work quite well for a number of schools.

In each case, both small and large schools, the school team is composed of representatives of various divisions within the school. The school team serves the following functions:

A. Addresses those issues that cross grade/department boundaries (attendance, support service delivery systems, schedules, and such).

B. Coordinates the work of the various grade/department groups.

C. At times, if an issue is compelling, directs the work of the grade/department groups (implementing a new writing or reading program, or directing a school-wide emphasis on higher order thinking skills, or improving the quality and quantity of feedback, or changing the grading structure, etc.)

In carrying out its work the school team follows essentially the same protocol described earlier. The team identifies a student performance issue(s), documents the issue(s) with data, and then proceeds to identify changes in adult practices that need to be implemented to change the students' level of performance. As the team carries out its work it is critical that the various division representatives maintain continuous two-way communication with their peers (see "Squeezing the Accordion" in the Appendix).

In the case of small schools, the representatives on the school team are drawn directly from the teachers teaching the same grade or class. In the case of the large schools the representatives on the school team are usually department heads since there are simply too many common course teams

140

to make a workable group. In the case of large schools each department becomes another team, coordinating the work of the department both internally and in concert with the work of the school team. This arrangement works well to create a common purpose and coordinated effort, while at the same time allowing each level to determine issues important to them.

In general it is best to leave identification of necessary instructional changes to those closest to the students. In both the small and large schools this would be the teacher teams, either grade level or common course. Unless the school or department team can make a compelling case for an instructional change that needs to take place, these teams should focus on structural issues that cross classroom boundaries. There have been numerous iterations of how this work is arranged and coordinated that have all worked well. Each school needs to create the system that works best for the unique context present in the school.

In both cases, small school and large school, the grade level or common course team serves the following functions:

A. Identify the most significant student performance issue and document it with data.
B. Identify the teacher practice that needs to be implemented at a high level to change the student outcome.
C. Implement the enhanced/new practice and measure both implementation and effect on student performance.

The work of the grade level/common course teams should be monitored by the school team and department teams respectively. Electronic record keeping has made this task efficient and effective. The teams simply record their progress on a shared site for all to see.

A complete discussion of all of the issues involved in the work and coordination of these various teams is beyond the scope of this book. For more detailed information the reader is referred to, "Harnessing the Power of Teacher Teams" (2014), by this author.

Stop

Your team is now at a critical juncture. You have learned about the documented benefits of moving to a more collaborative structure. You have learned some of the critical elements that must be included to make this structure truly effective. And you have learned of some of the real impediments you are likely to encounter as you attempt to implement this level of collaborative work in your district or school.

By now you must understand that to accomplish this task will take a tremendous effort on the part of the implementation team. Depending upon the current status of your district or school, this process will take a concerted commitment of at least 2 to 3 years. It is prudent at this point to ask a series of questions. The answers to these questions should help the team to decide whether or not to move forward.

1. Do we have the resources in terms of staff and time to carry through on this implementation?
2. Do we have the resources in terms of funding to support this initiative for several years?
3. Do the potential benefits in terms of improved student performance warrant this effort?
4. Are key people involved in this implementation likely to remain here for the time it will take?
5. Are the cultural/tradition changes that will be necessary to implement this level of collaborative work possible at this time?
6. Are we prepared to severely limit other initiatives while we implement this work in order to avoid "initiative overload"?

If after thinking deeply and honestly about the issues raised by these questions the team concludes that at this time it does not appear feasible to reach the level of implementation we feel would be necessary, it would be prudent to halt the process right here. There is nothing wrong about acknowledging that a district or school is just not ready at this time to move forward on such a significant change. More harm can be done by trying to implement a program and doing it poorly than by waiting until a more opportune time.

This author would recommend that the team develop a list of questions similar to those above. The members could then take a week or two to individually think about each question. Then come together to a meeting in which the group sees if there is consensus to answer the final question:

Based upon everything we know at this point, should we plan to move forward to implement high quality collaboration teams or not?

Developing an Implementation Plan

Planning for the Sustained Implementation of High Quality Collaborative Teams

Hopefully the proceeding pages armed your implementation team with enough information to begin to draft a plan to implement high quality collaborative teams in your school or district. Information however is just the beginning of the process. Being knowledgeable about the benefits and consequences of a practice will not insure that the practice is implemented effectively. Only through thoughtful, careful, sensitive, continuous and persistent implementation can a practice as powerful as high quality collaboration be successfully implemented. The following outline is designed to be used by the implementation team to begin to capture its thoughts as to how to proceed. As described in the Dynamic Planning Process earlier in this document, we cannot get too far ahead of ourselves with this planning. It is actually impossible to anticipate all of the problems and challenges that will arise during a multi-year implementation process such as this. But we can anticipate that these events will occur and create a structure designed to address each event as it occurs.

Since implementation of high quality collaboration structures in a school or district is actually a significant institutional change for most schools/districts, readers are referred to the work of John Kotter (Kotter, 2005). Kotter is one of this country's foremost experts on organizational change. This writer would suggest an investigation by the implementation team into some of Kotter's writing.

Kotter, John P. (2005). Our Iceberg is Melting. St.Martins Press.

Issues and Responses

Initiation

How will we deliver the information necessary for staff to understand the importance and effectiveness of high quality collaboration to everyone who needs it? What information needs to be shared in what sequence and with whom? What are the short-term needs and what are the long-term needs? How do we answer the question, "Why should I do this?"

_____

_____

_____

_____

_____

_____

_____

Organization

How do we organize out teams? Is it by grade level, department, common course, or interdisciplinary or some other configuration? Do we have different organizational schemes for different schools? Do we let each school decide the best scheme? Do we organize school teams first?

_____

_____

_____

_____

_____

_____

Training

How do we deliver the initial training to teams regarding best practice? How do we follow up that initial training? Do we provide coaches? Do we set up a blog or other communication device? Do we establish specific expectations with timelines for principals?

_____

_____

_____

_____

Follow-up

How do we follow up to the initial training? Do we expect our administrators to be responsible for implementation in their schools or teams? How do we define this? How do we monitor implementation? How do we integrate people new to the system?

_____

_____

_____

_____

_____

_____

Implementation Structure

How will we address the issue of changing staff? As new people enter the system (teachers, principals, central office staff) how will we insure that they are as knowledgeable as they need to be about the process? Since they have missed the initial and perhaps follow-up training, how will they acquire the information they need?

_____

_____

_____

_____

_____

_____

_____

Assessment

How will we assess progress teams are meeting? How frequently will these assessments occur? How will we respond to teams that are not making progress?

_____

_____

_____

_____

_____

_____

As an implementation team how often will we need to meet? How formal should our structure be? How are we going to create accurate communication with the schools in order to be aware of what is going on and be able to respond in a timely manner? How frequently will we need to go to each school? Should this be a formal or informal process?

_____

_____

_____

_____

_____

After having thought about these implementation issues we are ready to draft a plan covering the next month.

Within 30 School Days of This Date We Will Accomplish the Following:

Action	Target Date	Outcome

Closing Remarks

Hopefully, after reading this book and completing the reflection pieces members of the implementation team charged with moving their school or district toward a more collaborative environment are not discouraged.

Having gone through this process may have had a sobering effect on some. Moving toward more collaboration – real collaboration - involves a significant change in the culture of most schools and districts. Generations of isolated practice and a top down structure do not disappear overnight.

Yes, this is difficult work. Most things worth accomplishing are difficult. However, if the team concludes at this point that the time is not right to pursue this goal it would be a wise and courageous decision to stop. More damage in the long term can be caused by trying to implement a change that an organization is just not ready for at the moment.

If the decision is to go forward and support is needed this author is more than willing to offer any assistance deemed necessary.

Contact Information:

Email: michaelwasta@yahoo.com

Appendix

Appendix A

"The Futility of PLC Lite"

In this provocative article, authors Rick DuFour and Douglas Reeves point out that the collaborative process labeled Professional Learning Communities (PLC) frequently fails to live up to the expectations of what a PLC truly means. They point out that a true PLC knows explicitly what they expect their students to learn, accurately and frequently assess their learning, adjust their instruction when the evidence indicates they have not learned the material and provide meaningful assistance to those students struggling to learn.

As the authors point out, if any of these aforementioned activities are omitted the PLC is practicing PLC Lite. They go on to describe a series of unsuccessful practices that are often employed by groups describing themselves as PLC's, which undermine the potential benefits of the process. Among these practices are:

➤ Using assessments that are not formative or owned by the teachers and thus are of little use to guide their instruction
➤ Using data only to assign students to intervention and not as a basis for discussions of instructional practices
➤ Using data to publicly praise or humiliate principals and teachers
➤ Using inappropriate interventions based on data such as retention rather than changing instructional practices
➤ Using collaborative time to share "war stories" or discuss student behavior with no real change in practice

The authors conclude by urging professionals engaged in collaborative PLC work to use data from common formative assessments created by teachers to determine the specific effects of their teaching and analyze the data, not to humiliate teachers but as a way to improve the effectiveness of their instruction.

"The futility of PLC Lite" by Rick DuFour and Douglas Reeves in Kappan magazine, March 2016 (Vol. 97, # 6. p. 69 – 71).

Appendix B

"PLC's on Steroids"

In this article author Michael Wasta describes taking the work of collaborative PLC's to a new level. Based upon his work with hundreds of collaborative teams the author has moved teacher practice to the center of the PLC work. While still using student data to analyze student's learning, in this enhanced PLC work equal or more attention is paid to the instructional practices being employed by the teachers.

Rather than relying on vague descriptions of whatever practice or strategy teachers are employing to instruct students, these collaborative groups are identifying specific attributes of the practice or strategy associated with exemplary implementation and actually measuring the implementation in classrooms through observations or video. The discussions in their collaborative sessions move from almost exclusive talk about the students to talk about their understanding of and implementation of their practice. In these collaborative groups teachers are in effect designing and implementing their own professional development as they focus on a practice they have decided is important and are working as true professionals to improve that practice.

Throughout the process, teachers are taking frequent snapshots of performance (formative assessments) not only of the students but of their increasing efficacy in implementing the strategy. Thus they are armed with data documenting student progress and can relate that data to their improved instructional implementation.

"PLC's on Steroids" by Michael J. Wasta in Kappan magazine. February 2017 (Vol. 98, #5. P.67-71).

Appendix C

"Words Matter"

In this fascinating article, authors Genevieve Graff-Ermeling, Bradley A. Ermeling and Ronald Gallimore point out the problems caused when educators use vague or imprecise language to describe their practice.

Citing several examples from their coaching work with collaborative groups of teachers, the authors point out how when it comes to describing the practice they wish to employ, teachers frequently provide such superficial descriptions that they can each go their way thinking they are implementing the same practice, when observation reveals they are not even close to similar.

Some of the examples they cite are:

An Algebra team working on having students engage in a rich conceptual problem decided they would all "Share, discuss and analyze with the whole class." When asked by the coach what that discussion would look like the team began to realize that their description was so general and their ideas of "discussion" so different that more specificity was required.

An elementary team, having been trained in a specific strategy involving students as the agents of explanation in which over a third of the teachers reverted to teacher centered explanation concluded that the expectation that everyone understood a common meaning for "explain" proved to be an unwarranted assumption.

The authors offer four ways to assist teachers to become more precise in their descriptions of strategy;

1. Engage grade-level or subject –area team leaders in identifying and unpacking common and familiar terms used in lesson planning such as "explain".

2. Encourage teacher teams and individual teachers to hold a deliberate step in the lesson planning process where they identify and unpack words with multiple meanings.
3. Foster a habit of asking probing questions when discussing instructional practices with colleagues.
4. Become the novice and ask teachers to explain their ideas to you.

The authors conclude by extolling the value of well-defined and specified language in improving classroom interaction and creating opportunities to learn.

"Words Matter", by Genevieve Graff-Ermeling, Bradley A. Ermeling and Ronald Gallimore in Learning Forward. December 2015 (Vol. 36, # 6. P. 20-23).

Appendix D

"Accuracy of Teacher Reports of Their Classroom Behavior"

In this dated but important study authors Hook and Rosenshine looked at eleven studies in which the researchers attempted to measure the accuracy of teacher reports of their own classroom behavior. The results are interesting in that in the vast majority of cases the authors of the studies found a very low correlation between what the teachers recalled doing and what independent observers in these same classrooms recorded.

Going further it appeared that when the post observation questions were of a more general nature as to what happened in the classroom the correlations were higher but as the questions moved to more specific aspects of what the teacher was doing the correlations got weaker and weaker.

"Accuracy of Teacher Reports of Their Classroom Behavior", by Colin M. Hook and Barak V. Rosenshine in Review of Educational Research. Winter 1979 (Vol. 49 #1. P. 1-12).

Appendix E

"Squeezing the Accordion"

Whenever a team is making decisions that are going to affect other members of the staff it is critical in a truly collaborative setting that these other members have an opportunity to have their voices heard. This situation occurs most frequently when a school-wide team is contemplating taking action. The last thing that a team such as this wants is to have other staff members think that a "select" group is deciding things for them.

A strategy that has been found effective in situations such as these is "squeezing the accordion". Our colleague, Larry Ainsworth, suggested this strategy. Here is how it works.

When the team has a decision concerning some important action that will affect members of the staff not on the team the team will send that decision as a proposal to all who will be affected (Open the accordion). Everyone is asked to weigh in on the proposed decision within a defined period of time (not too much time). After everyone's feedback is received (squeeze the accordion) the team seriously reviews the feedback and modifies the proposal if deemed appropriate (if at all possible the team should find some way to tweak the proposal in response to the feedback). The proposal (revised hopefully) is sent again to everyone (open the accordion) with the direction that this will be the final opportunity to change the proposal. When the feedback is received (squeeze the accordion) the proposal is now finalized and implemented.

A true story will demonstrate the importance of this strategy and why it is worth the time.

> An elementary school team had been working on improving the Interactive Read Aloud (IRA) strategy used in the school's literacy program. The school team identified 12 elements of an IRA they felt needed to be present if the strategy were to meet their definition of exemplary. If any element was missing the implementation was not to be counted as exemplary. The team then sent this information to all teachers in the school charged with using the IRA strategy as part of their Reader's Workshop model. Every teacher sent written feedback concerning their opinion regarding the necessity of all 12 elements being present to meet the exemplary standard. There was 100% agreement that all 12 elements must be present.

Then the team started to collect implementation evidence. Each teacher was asked to video an IRA and score their implementation using a checklist of the 12 elements to determine if they were present or not. Not one teacher in the school had all 12 elements present. At this point several teachers said that they did not have certain elements because they didn't really think they were that important after all and thus wanted to count their implementation as exemplary even though one or more elements were absent. These teachers were reminded that they had all agreed that all 12 elements had to be present to count the implementation as exemplary and that they did not have the unilateral right to disregard the decision of the group. They were told that if they wished to come to the next team meeting and present an argument as to why certain elements should not be necessary to consider the lesson exemplary they were welcomed but in the meantime all 12 must remain. Not one teacher took the team up on its offer.

Within three months over 90% of the IRA lessons in this school were meeting the standard for exemplary implementation (all 12 elements) as defined by the team.

In the example just cited the issue of collaborative practice and private practice met head on. In the culture of most schools teachers will readily agree to certain standards of practice without much thought because when they get in their classrooms and close the door they will do what they want anyway. This does not seem to be done in a planned, obstinate manner. It is just that this is the way it has always been. In the absence of clear, agreed upon descriptions of a particular practice many teachers actually think they are doing what was agreed upon when objective observation reveals a very different thing.

Taking the time to "squeeze the accordion" a couple of times is well worth the effort. Moving from private practice to collaborative practice is not pain free. The more input people have into the process the more the pain can be eased.

ABOUT THE AUTHOR

Dr. Wasta has over four decades of experience working in schools, from the classroom to the Board Room. Currently he is a consultant affiliated with Creative Leadership Solutions in Boston, Massachusetts. He works with schools and districts on developing sustainable structures for effective collaborative practice in their school communities. He is the author of, <u>Harnessing the Power of Teacher Teams</u>, copyright 2014, which provides an innovative step by step approach to improve instruction for all students. By asking the people who know students best what is happening in classrooms, this model taps the expertise of teachers to reform schools.

Dr. Wasta lives with his wife in West Hartford Connecticut.

Email address: michaelwasta@yahoo.com

CPSIA information can be obtained
at www.ICGtesting.com
Printed in the USA
BVOW06s1916141217
502820BV00012B/558/P